My Awesome Explorer Field Guide

The Practical Kids Nature Guide: A Basic How-to-Survive and Be Prepared in the Wilderness Book with 30 Creative Projects to Spark Curiosity in the Outdoors

Copyright © 2019

Kim Fiona Atlas

"I believe that there is a subtle magnetism in Nature, which, if we unconsciously yield to it, will direct us aright."

-Henry David Thoreau

CONTENTS

INTRODUCTION

Nature is amazing. Just one look out the window and you can see a variety of birds, plants, and insects. Venture outdoors and a little way away from your home and you can find all sorts of animals making their homes not just in the woods, but in cities too.

Sound cool? Then you may be wondering if it's a good idea to take a day trip or even a weekend trip to the nearest park or camping ground with your family. The answer is yes! Not only will you get to enjoy the great outdoors and all that it has to offer, but you'll get to spend some fun time with your family away from the obligations of everyday life at home.

Before you run to Mom and Dad begging them to for a trip to the woods, though, there are some things you should know about surviving in the wilderness. We'll cover the easy stuff, like how to pack a basic first aid kit, and more serious things like how to build a shelter and how to navigate with a compass. Have your parents or guardian read this book with you so they know all this important information, too.

Ready? Let's get started!

CHAPTER 1: Safety First

Respect Nature

The most important rule to remember when out in the wilderness is "Respect Nature." In the wilderness we are bound to see, and get a bit too close to, wild animals. As cool as these creatures are, they don't like humans bothering them. Sometimes humans carry germs that can make these animals very sick. Others are endangered and should be left in peace so they can have a better chance of survival.

Plants should be respected as well. Some are poisonous, and others have tiny stingers that will hurt very badly if they get into in your skin. Some plants are endangered, too, and like animals they should be left alone so they have the best chance for survival.

The bottom line is that whenever you are out in the wild (even if that's just in the park near your home), it's best to respect Nature by keeping your hands to yourself, paying attention to your surroundings and watching where you step. DO NOT put yourself or others in danger if you can avoid it at all.

What to Do if You Get Lost

Even when you know where you are going, it can be easy to get distracted or turned around. Suddenly you realize that you don't know where you are – you're lost! What to do?

First rule: Don't panic. No really, don't panic. It's scary to get lost, especially if you're in an area you're not familiar with. However, it's important to stay calm because panic can lead you to making bad decisions that can get you hurt or worse.

An old piece of advice that still gets offered is to stay in one place until someone finds you. It's a good idea, but in order for it to work, people need to know where you'll be and what day and time you should be back home. This is why it's smart to tell people who you trust what your plans are, especially if you're going somewhere new. They'll know where you're supposed to be and can let emergency services know where to start looking for you.

If you're very far from a trail, campground, or other landmark that would make it easier for people to find you, then it's time to use some of the safety equipment you brought with you. See the chapter titled "How to Pack a Survival Kit" for a list of items to include in your pack.

Clothes and Other Items

Being outdoors can be lots of fun, but it's better when you dress right for the weather where you'll be going, and even more important in a survival situation. The right clothing and equipment can do a lot to keep you comfortable. Here are some tips:

- Before you leave on a trip, check the weather forecast. While the forecast can't keep track of every change in weather that may happen, you can still get a good idea of what to bring and what to wear. A survival situation will be easier to bear with the right clothes.

Learn about the area that you will be visiting, including the wildlife and plant life. In a survival situation, knowledge about the world around you will help with finding food and water, where to build a shelter, etc.

- If you're going to be out in the sun a lot, remember to wear sunscreen and bring plenty of water. Whether you wear short sleeves or long sleeves, sunscreen is important for reducing your chances of getting sunburn and otherwise damaging your skin. Drinking plenty of water or even a sports drink is important to avoid dehydration.

If you're going to be going outdoors when it is cold, wear layers. This method was developed by the US Army, and the reason it has remained an important piece of advice is because IT WORKS. It's much easier to cool down by removing one or two layers while still keeping yourself protected; when you start to get cold, you can add just enough layers to keep yourself warm but not make yourself too hot and uncomfortable.

- If there's a chance for bad weather, bring the right jacket for it. If it might rain, bring a waterproof or water-resistant jacket. If it might snow, bring a jacket just heavy enough to provide some protection when put on over your clothes.

If you think rain will be present throughout your trip, you can try adding a pair of gaiters or rain pants to your gear. Gaiters are garments worn over your shoes and the lower pant legs. They used to be made of leather, but nowadays are made of synthetic material. These are great if you are concerned about snow, mud, etc. entering the top of your boots as you move around but want to avoid wearing another full layer over your pants. They can offer some protection against snakebites, too.

- Rain pants are what they sound like: pants designed to keep the wearer dry when rain falls for hours or even days. They are usually worn over another pair of pants, especially if you need both warmth and water protection. However, some people will wear their rain paints alone, if they find it comfortable enough to do so. There has been more than one heated discussion about which way is the proper way, the best way, but in the end it is up to you to decide what you prefer.
-When layering your clothes, make sure to use clothes that will keep you dry and comfortable. If you have room in your pack, bring extra clothes. Not only will you have clean clothes in the event that the ones you wear need to be cleaned or thrown away, spare clothing can be

used for other things (to filter water or tie a splint, for example).

- Protect your eyes. Ideally, wear sunglasses that are rated to protect your eyes from both UVA and UVB light. If you have a pair that you can change the lenses on, remember to bring those extra lenses and the carrying case. A change in light levels can make some lenses too dark for you to see or let in too much light.

If you lose your sunglasses or they get broken, you can improvise by making your own. Cut a strip of cloth, tree bark, etc. to fit over your eyes like a mask. Cut narrows slits for your eyes. The slits must be big enough for you to see through yet let in as little light as possible. Apply soot under your eyes to reduce glare, otherwise you risk the sun's ultraviolet (UV) light burning the surface of your eyes from below, as it reflects of sand, snow, and water. Tie your makeshift sunglasses in place with string or cord, or anything strong and flexible enough to act as cord.

- Have a proper first-aid kit with you. Make sure that if you or someone else uses an EpiPen or medication that you have these things on hand, and replace expired supplies as needed.

A word about clothes: When layering, make sure the clothes which will be touching your skin will help to direct sweat away from your body. (If you're only wearing one layer, this is still something you should keep in mind – sweaty clothes can irritate skin.) The second layer needs to be something that will help keep you warm without weighing you down, and will still keep you from getting soaked with sweat. The third layer should be one that protects you from wind, rain, etc., so something like a rain jacket or a wind-resistant jacket would work; an insulated one would be ideal for extremely cold climates.

- Wear proper footwear. Hiking boots will work for most rough terrain, though you may have to double up on socks if the weather turns very cold. For rainforests or swampy land, you want boots which have vents for expelling water from inside – this will help keep your feet dry and comfortable. For desert regions, you want boots that are light enough to keep your feet from getting too hot, but sturdy enough to withstand wear and tear and protect your feel and ankles from snake bites. Bring snowshoes if you will be traveling through a snowy region.

In a pinch, you can make snowshoes out of pine branches. Find two densely needled branches of equal size, about 2.5 to 3 feet long. Tie a long cord or some strong grasses around the thickest part of each branch, about an inch or two from the end. Check that there's enough cord or rope loose to attach your boot to the branch.

Loop the cord on both sides underneath the first boughs on each branch. Place your foot on the body of the branch, closest to the end where the knot is tied. Tie your boot into place by looping the cord around you toe and heel, and tying it securely.

- Have a hat with you. Besides shielding your face and neck from the sun, a hat also helps to keep your head warm and protects you from rain, snow, and sleet. A cold, wet head may not cause a cold but it's no fun to deal with!

A plain baseball cap may work fine for a hike on a clear day, but it's not the best choice for wet weather unless you pair it with a rain jacket (the bill keeps the rain out of your face so you can see). Your best bet is a wide-brimmed hat so that both your face and the back of your neck have some protection from the sun (the color and overall style of hat is up to you). Colder temperatures call for a hat that's made for such conditions. A knit cap would be fine on its own, but can also be worn under another hat that's waterproof if there is rain; it also provides extra warmth under a jacket hood. You can get one of those caps with ear flaps if you think it's going to get very cold, below freezing even.

- Bring a pocketknife and a sharpener. Keep your knife clean and sharp. It's one of the most valuable tools a person can have in a survival situation. You can bring another knife, such as a Bowie, kukri or a machete, but a pocketknife (a Swiss Army knife being the most popular choice) is still good to have.

An ax. There are a wide variety of axes on the market. Some are the classic double-bitted ax that many people think of when you say the word "ax" and others are more like mutlitools. What model you pick will depend on what you're looking for. Some swear by the survival axes that can be used as shovels and other tools and some prefer to stick with just an ax, and buy other tools as needed. Some will be heavier than others so it might be best to visit a store which sells axes and try holding a few. This will help you figure out which ones won't be a lot of trouble for you to lift and swing, and you'll get an idea of what to look for if you choose to buy an ax online.

- If you bring a sleeping bag, bring one that is designed for the weather conditions you expect to endure. Different styles are best for different temperatures and weather. Generally speaking, sleeping bags are separated in three basic categories: summer, winter, and three-season.

Winter: These bags are best for use in temperatures of 20°F and below. They have hoods that you can pull close and tight around your head, draft collars (an extra tube of fabric stuffed with insulation, found just below the hood, mean to wrap around your chest and shoulders to trap warm air), and zipper draft tubes (these block drafts from sneaking their way through the zipper). They are well-stuffed with insulation which can be down (those fine feathers you find beneath the heavier, water-shedding feathers on birds) or synthetic.

Summer: For temperatures of 30°F and higher, these lightweight bags are your best choice. Because they don't have as much insulation as winter bags, they pack down tiny which makes they very portable. They often have full-length zippers, allowing you to open them completely for better ventilation or to use as a quilt on night when it's too hot to use a closed sleeping bag.

Three-season: Rated best for using at temperatures of about 20°F and above, these are best for spring and fall trips. If you're heading to the high mountains in the summer, a bag of this type would work to keep you warm when nighttime temperatures drop to freezing. The best three-season bags have extra features to combat colder temperatures, features that are often found in winter bags as well.

To make things a bit more complicated, sleeping bags come in different shapes. Each shape has its pros and cons. Which one you pick will depend on what you need and the environment you'll be in.

A word on waterproofing: only get a waterproof bag if you tend to camp without a tent or live where wet conditions are a regular feature of the weather. Note that you'll pay more for a waterproof shell. Check that the fabric will still breathe, or else you'll be sleeping in a puddle of your own sweat.

Now, to the bag shapes:

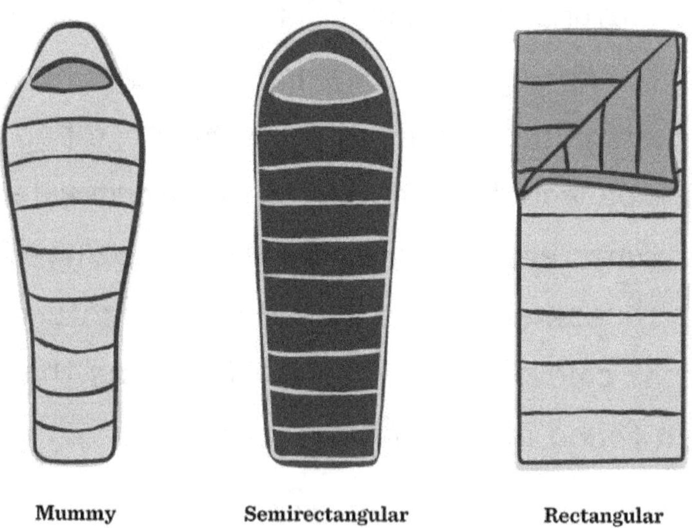

Mummy   Semirectangular   Rectangular

Mummy-style sleeping bags – good for cold weather conditions. These cover all but your face, trapping as much body heat as possible to keep you warm. They're tapered through the legs and feet for maximum thermal efficiency – the smaller the interior space of a sleeping bag, the more heat it can trap. Restless sleepers and those bigger bodies may find this shape too confining and uncomfortable. Mummy bags are also lighter in weight since they use less material and insulation, so they pack small.

Rectangular – the classic sleeping bag shape. These are not as thermally efficient as other shapes, so are best suited for backyard campouts and indoor sleepovers. You can probably use these bags with a tent and a sleeping pad on a camping trip away from home, but not if you expect the temperature to drop or if there will be rain or snow.

Semi-rectangular: This bag is a happy medium between mummy and rectangular shapes.

It's a good choice for people who hate the confining shape of a mummy bag but need more warmth than a rectangular bag can offer. These bags give you more room to roll around and thrash about, but they are bulkier and heavier than mummy bags.

A few more things you should know: Try out a few sleeping bags to find one that's comfortable and is the right size. If it comes with a sleeve for a sleeping pad, try it out that way in the store to check the fit. Read the care instructions which come with your sleeping bag and follow them. A well-cared for sleeping bag will last you many trips, possibly adding up to several years' worth of use.

- Sleeping pads and cots are optional, but they can offer a bit more comfort when sleeping. Sleeping pads come in three basic types: 1) closed-cell foam, the "old school" stuff, 2) self-inflating, also rather old school, and 3) air construction, which is the type most commonly found these days. Each type has its strengths and weak points.

Closed-cell foam: This is probably what many thinks of when they think of sleeping pads for camping. They're not the most comfortable option, but they make up for that in durability. Closed-cell foam doesn't pop. It can rip, tatter, ribbon, or even shred, but chances are a closed-cell foam pad will still be usable. On the upside, these pads are generally lightweight and fairly inexpensive. Their durability makes them a great choice to pair with an inflatable pad to add extra warmth and ground protection.

Self-inflating: These pads use an open-celled foam (think of a kitchen sponge) layered between two pieces of fabric. Open the valve on the pad, and the foam expands and inflates the pad. It traps air and retain heat as well. The process takes around five minutes for a new pad, but old ones will take longer because the foam becomes compressed with repeated use. Thus it's best to store this type of pad semi-inflated and not compressed, to extend the life of the foam.

Air Construction: Go down to the camping store and prepared to be dazed and confused by how many options there are to choose from. These pads are usually very plush, lightweight, and come in a variety of insulation levels. The downside is that these aren't the most durable sleeping pads around. They are, after all, only laminated fabric filled with air. Put a grown adult on this, and sooner or later the stress will cause air leaks. If you want to invest in this type of pad, then also invest in a patch kit with additional repair patches, superglue, and rubber cement.

And now, tents! No wilderness exploration guide would be complete without a section about tents. There's so much to know and consider when buying a tent that it seemed fair to have a whole section of this guide dedicated to them.

Ever since humans first started traveling from place to place for longer than a few hours, one of the biggest problems we faced was "Where am I going to sleep for the night?" You can't always count on there being a cave, or that a cave is not already home to a bear or another wild animal. In truth, it is simply not sensible to rely on nature always providing the right kind of shelter. It made more sense for humans to start constructing our own shelters that we could bring with us when we traveled.

It's from this idea that the tent, that most classic of camping items and an image so well-known that it's used on road signs to indicate where camping sites are found, was born. (And RVs, but those came much later, after motor vehicles became commonplace and someone probably wondered, "Hey, how hard would it be to combine a truck and a house into one unit?") Humans needed something portable, something lightweight, that could be taken apart and

packed up for transport on foot, on a sled of
some sort, or on the back of a domesticated
animal. Ever since the first tent, probably just an
animal hide or two supported by sticks, was
invented, humans have improved and expanded
upon that basic setup. The result is that we have
seen, and continue to see, a variety of tents
being sold and used.

We'll go over the tents you're most likely to see in the store and, just for fun, a few which are less common outside of certain parts of the world. If you travel abroad, though, you may get the chance to use one of them.

- **Ridge tent**: The most basic of tents. It gets the name from the fact that it has a cross pole, a ridge pole, holding up the roof, creating that characteristic raised edge in the center of the roof. Ridge tents are remarkably stable, which is probably why we see them ranging in size from one-person tents to large marquees that you see at wedding and festivals. They're easy to pitch as well.

The main disadvantage of these tents lies in the head height. Even the largest units have limited height. This isn't a problem if the tent is to be used for sleeping, but for a family gathering in the rain or some other event, it's better if the tent's design allows you to move freely about inside.

-**Dome tent**: These tend to have the basic shape of a half-circle. However, the actual shape of the dome varies depending on how many flexible poles make up the frame supporting it. Two poles crossing in the middle give a square dome, three will get you a hexagon. Overall headroom is better across a wider floor area due to the side being more vertical, and these tents have very good stability in smaller sizes. And that's the darwback: the bigger the dome, the less stable it is.

-**Gedodesic and semi-geodesic**: "Geodesic" is a mathematical term, originally meant to indicated a line that was the shortest route between two points on earth. Now, it;s used to describe a tent where the poles crisscross over the sruface and form triaangles at their intersections. Having multiple points of failure, spreading out the stress on the tent, makes it the most stable type of tent for extreme weather conditions. Ever look at a picture of people making camp on Mt. Everest or somewhere else with extreme weather? Check the tents – chances are you'll see a lot of geodesic tents.

Semi-geodesic tents are similar, but use fewer poles and are suited for slightly less extreme conditions. They share the vaunted stability of full geodesic tents. They're normally produced in smaller sizes for those who are likely to pitch them in windy, exposed terrain or on mountainsides.

-**Quick-pitch or instant tents**: These are the latest in a range of tents that really do pitch themselves. You have a long, coiled, sprung frame permanently fitted into the fabric of the tent. Twist the frame, and the tent becomes a circular package.

Unleash the spring – if you want to be dramatic, you can do this by throwing the whole lot into the air – and the sprung frame turns the fabric bag into an elegant and practical shelter. Fun to watch! Easy to transport, too.

People used to say these tents were only suitable for good weather conditions. Recent developments have led to much more robust models. Some have inner tents and sleeping space for as many as five people. Many are still best kept for a night or two at a festival, or for kids to use while having a backyard campout.

-**Inflatable tents**: Rare, but most people have heard of them. And they are exactly what the name indicates. All you need to do is to lay out the tent, peg the corners down, and turn on the included compressor. In just a few minutes there will be a full-sized tent standing in place – with hardly any work on your part! They are one of the more expensive options, though, and despite needing only air to get them ready for use, they are surprisingly heavy.

-**Khyam tent**: This name is well-known in the world of "instant tents." Khyam's system is based on a simple sprung "knuckle" or elbow joint. It can hold a flexible pole straight or be 'broken' to let the pole bend. As with other instant tents, the skeleton is permanently fitted to the fabric. Getting the tent set up is very easy: Take it out of the bag and let the poles fall into the right position. Working your way around the tent, the poles are straightened using the elbow joints so that the final shape is achieved. Just avoid pinching your finger.

-**Tunnel tent**: The name says it all. Flexible poles are bound into semi-circles and stood up in a line to create a tunnel. Other tents use sturdy, rigid poles to form the structure. Tunnel tents come in a staggering variety of sizes and styles. They are the most common form of family tents seen in campsites.

-**Vis-a-vis**: Once tunnels and domes got bigger, designers thought to add extra rooms to the basic structure. This started in France, where you'd find tents with a large central part that would offer standing headroom, and an annex room off to each side where sleeping compartments were located. These compartments faced each other, thus the French term "vis-a-vis." These tents can be domes or tunnels, though some of the very first ones were square frame tents.

-**Pod style**: These are some of the latest large tent models on the market. They have a central living area with several sleeping areas (pods) leading off. Think of spokes spread out from the hub on a wheel.

In the family setting, children can have their own spaces. The central living space acts as a family gathering room. It's almost like a house.

This style has its flaws. You need a lot of ground area, and many campsites will charge extra for it. If pod tents are allowed on site at all. They also include a large volume of fabric than a tunnel tent of the same size, which makes them heavier to transport and more challenging to erect. If you like the pod arrangement but don't always need all the pods, look for a model that will let you pitch just some of the pods, leaving the unused ones at home.

-Large family tents: Designers love to try and scale up their favorite small tent shapes into bigger family tents. This doesn't always work out well. Some designs don't do well in smaller or bigger sizes – some very unstable giant dome tents have been produced, to the dismay of many.

As a general rule, tunnels work better in bigger sizes but if the wind catches them before they are properly pegged out, you'll have a nice big kite to wrestle with. Whoops!

Most manufacturers have realized there's a better way. They now produce tents which are a combination of styles, and they often work well. You could sleep in a dome and have a tunnel for the living area, for example.

-Frame tents: Flexible poles may reign, but there's still a place for the traditional rigid frame tent. In fact, they're still a popular choice.

These use a rigid framework of straight poles (usually steel) that have angled joints. They can offer lots of space including good headroom, and are very stable when properly set up. Frame tents tend to be heavier, though. They can take somewhat longer to erect than other tents.

-**Single pole tents**: These are based on the traditional tepee or the bell tent. They're enjoying a surge in popularity, so manufacturers have each introduced their take on this design in recent years. Single-pole tents look great on site, but a lack of inner tents mean most are best suited for 'fine weather' camping or festivals. There are exceptions, though.

-**Trailer tents**: Yes, you read that right. A trailer crossed with a tent. Many are large enough that you need a car or truck to tow them, but some are small enough to be towed behind a motorcycle. Perhaps the main difference between these and folding campers is that they need to be pegged out, whereas folding campers don't require pegs to be used.

-**Cabin tents**: These are usually made up of aluminum poles that fit together to create the frame of something that looks, well, like a cabin! They are often divided into room with internal dividers, making them a fine option for family camping. Sometimes there's a waterproof polyester, nylon or canvas rainfly encasing the frame to form the walls and roof of the unit. This setup provides plenty of living space that you can stand up in.

Fairly cheap in price, but also in quality. Cabin tents are also heavy and complicated to set up. They aren't known for their ability to withstand bad weather, so they are ideal for fair weather camping.

Time for a trip around the world! Some of these tents will be familiar and others may be new to you.

-**Yurt**: A versatile type of tent, as there is not just one kind. Traditionally used by people living the steppes of Asia. Yurts are most commonly associated with Mongolia. They can range from simple sheepskin constructions to large dwellings that have a permanent foundation and have furniture.

-**Tupiq**: A traditional type of tent used by the Inuit First Nations people, who live very far to the north. Years ago, the tupiq would be made out of sealskin, as that was the only material available that was thick enough to provided the needed insulation during the harsh winter. There are several different designs, based on size, as there were family tents and individual version of such. All of them were conical in shape. These days the Inuit use canvas tents, called *tupikhaq*.

-**Kohte**: One of the more interesting designs in Western Europe, this traditional tent is used by the German boy scouts. It is recognizable due to the unique shape of the four pnels that make it up, and the jet black color. The kohte was inspired by the lavvu.

-**Lavvu**: This tent is used by the Sami people of Finland and in adjoining regions. It's a lot like the teepee in its construction, featuring a skin wrapped around a cone of supporting poles which are forked and notches to keep them together. This is designed to be a temporary dwelling, as it can be broken down and taken to the next site. The notable difference between a lavvu and a teepee lies in the shape and the way the material is cut. Also, the lavvu is lower to the ground and wider than a teepee.

CHAPTER 2: Building a Shelter

Choose a location

You have many options for building a shelter depending on what materials you have and how long you think you will be out in the wilderness. If you have a tent with you, then the most you have to worry about is finding the right spot to pitch (set up) your tent:

-Avoid pitching a tent near a dead tree or under dead tree limbs.

-Don't pitch it near an animal burrow or a trail that's used by animals. You don't want to wake up in the middle of the night and find an unwelcome visitor in your tent.

-Avoid wet ground or ground that may get soaked or flooded in a storm.

-Don't pitch your tent downstream from a latrine.

-Pitch your tent on flat ground. Avoid low ground, though, because it collects cold air at night and may be home to lots of insects.

-Find a spot with sturdy natural windbreaks such as trees, or artificial windbreaks like walls of snow

-Stay out of the path of potential rockfalls, avalanches, and mud slides.

Stick to these guidelines and you should be fine.

And

If you have no tent, then you need to take into account the weather and what materials are available. A simple lean-to built of sticks and covered with leafy branches or a tarp would be enough in pleasant weather; for bad weather, you're going to need something sturdy and weatherproof. This is easiest when there's snow – snow is a great insulator and besides building a snow cave, you can also make a trench shelter in snow. Don't be afraid to leave these shelters standing when you leave. By doing so, you may help save the life of someone else who's lost.

You can dig a trench shelter in snow if you need something that doesn't require too much work. It's a great option for when the snow isn't much more than a foot deep, or it's not snow that you can pack. Pick an open space with plenty of snow and room for you to dig. Check the ground where you plan to put the trench by using a shovel or stick to look for logs or big rocks buried under the snow. Note that while you are doing this you're also marking where the walls of the trench will be, so don't walk anywhere else or you'll ruin the walls.

Dig a trench about 1-1/2 times the length of your body. Keep the sides as straight as you can and try to dig right down to the ground; if the snow is thick, dig down about three feet. If there's not a lot of snow, pile the snow that you dig out along the side to make the walls higher.

Now break some sticks around three feet long. You want ones that are about as wide as a ruler because they'll be bearing the weight of some snow. Arrange these over the top of your trench. Find evergreen boughs, break them off, and lay them in a thick layer over the sticks. Cover this roof with more snow, but don't put it too close to the walls; you need only a half foot to a foot of snow.

You need to put a thick layer of evergreen boughs on the bottom of the trench. This will keep you off the cold ground and provide a more comfortable spot to sleep. Last of all, block most of the entrance off with more snow so that warm air stays inside. You can put a stick through the roof to make sure there is ventilation even if the entrance gets completely blocked with snow during a storm. You're all done!

If you are lost and don't know how long you'll have to wait for help, you need something which will protect you from sun, rain, snow, and wind, and wild animals. In snowy regions, an igloo would do fine. As mentioned above, snow is some of nature's best insulation material. Find a hard, dry pile of snow and cut blocks from it. Using that hole where you cut the blocks as a guide, arrange the snow blocks in a spiral. You'll want to make a hole under the wall for an entrance and cold air sink. (Cold air is denser than warm or hot and it will sink rather than rise.) Once the igloo is finished, cut some air holes into the walls so that fresh air will enter the shelter.

Another option is to make a quinze (kwin-zee): place backpacks and other equipment in a tight cone, and pile snow on top. Leave the first layer for 30 minutes so it can harden before adding another layer. Add snow in this manner until you have about 3 feet of snow in the pile. Gather some long sticks and push them into the snow so they point to the center of the quinze. Start digging a hole at the bottom of one side of the pile work your way to the center. Once you find the center, dig out the snow until you see the ends of the sticks in the roof. See image below for an idea of how the process goes.

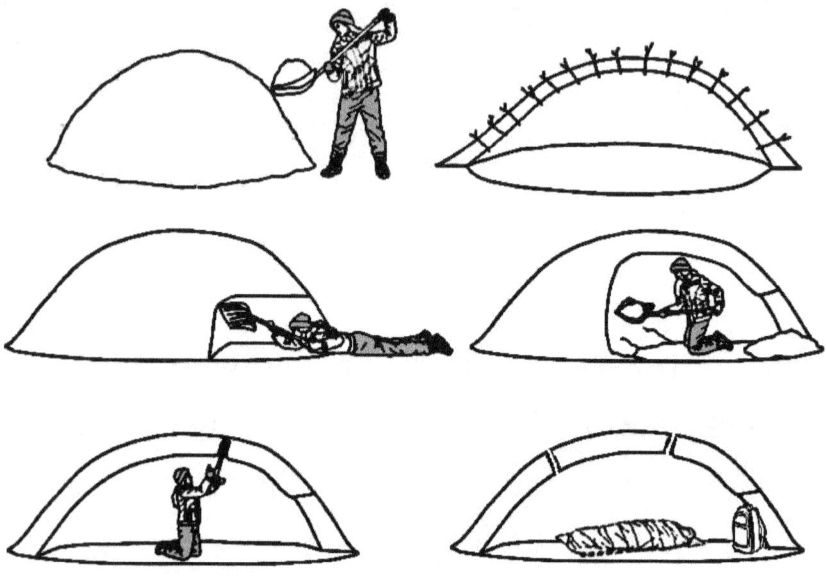

If you are in a region where there is no snow, you can try sheltering in a natural hollow or a cave. Make sure these places are not already occupied by animals and that they are solid and immovable. If that's not an option, you'll need to build a log cabin or perhaps a sod house. Both of these take time to build, so don't try unless you are certain that you will need long-term shelter.

To build a log cabin, you will need, obviously, logs. The type of wood you use is important, as they can shrink as they weather. In a survival situation you may have to look around and make do with whatever is available, even if it's not the best type of wood to use. You want logs which are straight, are the same length, and do not have large holes in them. Make sure you have enough logs to build the size cabin you want.

Clear the ground at least three feet beyond the walls of the cabin site. Mark the outline of the cabin with some logs. Oh, and to make sure these will stay in place, cut notches in the top and bottom ends. The logs will fit together like pieces of a jigsaw puzzle. Make sure the notching leaves each log squarely on top of the rest as you build up the walls.

Bear in mind that blank rear walls and the slope of the roof (this is important, we'll explain why later) should face prevailing winds and bad weather. The front door and any windows should face the sun. Make sure the logs used for the door fame are securely in place, as they also support the weight of the roof. The reason you should make the roof slope is for rain and snow to run off (easier than trying to add gutters or just letting the rain drip).

Once you've got the logs for the roof in place, it is time to lay on the roofing material. Just as if you were building a house, you need insulation, such as bracken, fir branches, grass, whatever you can find. If you find any stray pieces of man-made materials such as plastic sheeting, those would work; you can even try layering the grass or bracken over the plastic sheeting. Ideally, the outer layer of the rood should be made of thick sod. As a finishing touch, caulk between the logs of your cabin with mud and moss.

You could add a stone chimney to your cabin. The easiest way to do it would be to cut a hole in the back wall and, using rocks or mud bricks that you have dried in the sun, build the chimney outside and around the hole. Or you can stick with using a fire ring located outside the cabin.

A sod house is possible only if you are in an area where there is an abundant supply of turf which can be used. Assuming you are, the next concern is whether you will have the time and energy to do the job. If you do, then start as soon as possible.

Cut a section of sod from the ground. No need to dry these bricks – they'll work just fine as is. Lay an outline of your house on cleared, level ground. Leave a hole for the door. Make sure the ground will be able to take the considerable weight of the walls and roof without sinking.

Start building up the walls. Just like if you were building a brick house, lay each piece of sod over the joint of the two below it. Ensure that you do this consistently, and the walls should be firm and not topple. Try to keep them straight, at 90-degree angles to each other.

Build the front of the house than the back – a sloped roof will allow rain to run off into the wind. Don't forget to add a door frame; the lintel must be strong enough to bear the weight of several rows of sod bricks. Make a roof framework of sturdy branches if you have any available. Otherwise you're going to have to figure out how to pieces the roof together from whatever you have.

Place a layer of sods over the roof frame, grass facing upwards. Patch any cracks in the walls with mud. Here's the beauty of using sod: After weathering, the walls will become hard and smooth with no extra work on your part.

Properly made and cared for, a sod house will keep you cool in summer and warm during the winter. They can last six or seven years. Hopefully you're not lost for that long!

If you are in a tropical area, where it tends to get very hot and humid, you need a shelter which will protect you from rain, wind, and sun. In rainforests you must sleep off the ground, high enough that small animals can pass beneath you and heavy rain does not constantly splash you as it hits the ground. A mosquito net and a waterproof are vital for a tropical shelter.

A simple A-frame shelter is the easiest type to make. Cut seven long branches and tie two of them to a sturdy tree. Make a second A-frame and set it at a distance of about 2 feet longer than your height. Set a lightweight branch across the two top V's of the A-frames. This is the support pole for the roof.

Tie the sides of a groundsheet or some other material to make tubes. Inset two long poles and pull them apart to make a stretcher. Wedge this between the A-frames with the poles on the outside.

Stretch a waterproof tarp or some other waterproof covering across the ridge pole. Pull it tight on either side and tie to trees. The roof needs to keep rain off you but still have enough height to let air circulate around your head.

You can make a different kind of shelter that is better suited to keeping torrential rain off you. Make a frame that looks like a bed frame, with four posts hammered into the ground – these are the corner posts. Make them spaced just a little more than you are tall. Attach four branches between the posts lash them securely into notches that you made on the outside of the corner posts. Weave smaller branches across the frame to make a bed.

Make roof frame by tying seven branches together so they form a triangle that's open at the bottom. Tie this to the top of the corner posts. Tie more branches to the roof frame and then hang large leaves over them. Overlap the leaves so they don't let water leak in. Make sure the shiny side of the leaves is facing outward, the better to deflect rain.

Whatever your shelter, make sure to build it on level ground, just close enough to water and fuel sources. Food sources shouldn't be located too far away either. As with pitching a tent, look out for dangers like dead trees, branches, rockslides, etc. You may need to repair or modify it so that it will last longer and keep you better-protected from wild animals and foul weather.

CHAPTER 3: Avoiding Dangerous Animals

While part of the fun of being outdoors is seeing wild animals, there are many that you should avoid. No one wants to risk getting hurt by a big animal or bitten by a snake or spider. This is a huge concern when in a survival situation as you must take your safety into your own hands.

Keeping a safe distance between you and large animals is key. They may not notice you, or if they do, they may decide you aren't a threat since you're keeping well away. Not getting close means that both of you have the chance to leave without getting hurt.

It's a good idea to make noise as you are walking around. It cuts down on the chances of an animal being taken by surprise and attacking because it feels threatened. Talk or sing. If you have a walking stick, use it to rustle leaves on the ground or make other noise.

If you find you have gotten too close to a dangerous animal by accident, back away slowly and give it plenty of room. You may even speak in a soothing voice as a further sign that you don't mean harm. Sometimes though, an animal will still feel threatened and attack.

Bears: Keep as far away as possible. If a bear attacks (particularly a black bear) in a predatory manner, fight back. You must put up enough of a fight that the bear decides to try its luck with easier prey. Playing dead will work if you're being attacked by, say, a mother grizzly trying to protect her cubs. It's a good idea to carry bear spray – just make sure to aim it downwind of you so that the moving air will not blow it back into your eyes.

Pigs and Boars: **In** general, it is best to avoid these animals, as they can be very aggressive and can

do much damage in a fight. If you find yourself in a face-off, climb the nearest tree, car, boulder, etc. Get at least 6 feet the ground to discourage the pig from following you. If that's not an option, try to sidestep as quickly as you can to avoid getting gored by a pig's tusks as it charges. If you must fight, use whatever means possible to do so, and try to remain standing. This will help you avoid serious injury. You probably wont' have to fight for long – most wild pig attacks on humans last about a minute.

WOLVES and COYOTES: These animals may look alike to many, but make no mistake: they are very different and they compete with each other for food and territory. That being said, wolves tend to be more wary of humans and attacks on humans are rare. Many coyotes have readily adapted to living around humans to one degree or another, and this familiarity is one reason why they can be so dangerous.

If you see a wolf, stay calm. Do not run. Back away slowly while maintaining eye contact. Should the wolf begin to act aggressive (hackles raise, tail held high, howling or snarling), yell and throw things at it while backing away. If it attacks, fight back as hard as you can to show that you are not easy prey.

This advice also applies to coyotes.

If you happen to have a dog with you, DO NOT let them approach the wolf or coyote. Keep the dog close to you at all times (if you haven't got a proper leash, make one from a piece of rope, or try to find something else strong enough and flexible enough that you can tie it to your dog's collar or harness). If you must, place yourself between the two animals – this should end the encounter soon enough.

Moose and Deer: These animals are as dangerous as they are majestic. A full-grown moose can be hit with a car and survive – the car may not! Deer, though smaller, can do grave harm with their antlers and sharp hooves.

Moose can be aggressive any time of the year, but the risk of attack

increases during certain seasons. In late spring/early summer, female moose (cows) will be traveling with their young calves and attack if they feel their offspring are in danger. Fall is breeding season and during this time males (bulls) become competitive and very agitated. Finally, during the winter moose can become much more aggressive due to hunger and tiredness. If you've ever tried walking through deep snow for a long time, then you have some idea of how the moose feel!

If you do happen upon a moose at any time of the year, look for these clues that it may attack:

-The moose stops eating, drinking, etc. and stares directly at you.

- Hair on its hump, neck, or hips rises and its ears lay flat

-Licks or smacks its lips and clicks its teeth

-Urinates

-Lowers its head and walks toward your

-Whites of its eyes can be seen

-Whips its head back and forth like a horse does to show aggression

That being said, sometimes the moose shows all these signs but does not attack. In that case, sigh with relief and then get away quickly! Don't be tempted to get close, yell and whoop, or otherwise act foolish, just because the animal didn't charge at you. The moose may decide you are a threat after all and then you will need to think fast in order to save your life!

Deer may be smaller and more timid, but they are no less aggressive when they feel they are in danger, or that their babies are in danger. As with all wild animals, the best way to avoid an attack is to avoid getting too close and putting the deer in a situation where it decides that attacking you is the best choice. Keep your distance, and move away if you find that you've wandered too close. Just like moose, deer become much more aggressive during breeding season or when they have babies to protect. Exercise extreme caution in both cases.

It's actually a good idea to turn away and retreat – deer are less likely to give chase, and so attacks are less likely than if you stand your ground or move towards the deer. If all else fails, shout or make other noise and try to make yourself look bigger. If you're attacked anyway, put something between you and the deer such as a large stick or a backpack; this will put a bit of distance between you and the deer, and will lower your chances of getting hurt by its hooves or antlers. Continue to try to leave the area, or climb a tree and wait until the deer leaves.

Should the deer knock you down, curl up in the fetal position and keep your neck, head and vital organs covered. Even if you stay standing, you must protect your head, neck and face! In rare instances, the deer may be extremely aggressive and not stop attacking. You're going to have to fight back. Try to ruin the attack by grabbing the antlers or front legs and pushing the deer off-balance. Do whatever you can to make the deer realize you're not an easy target and keep going until the deer leaves or gets tired out.

The good news is that even as deer and humans come into contact more often, attacks are pretty rare. Let's help keep it that way by giving the animals space and treating them with respect.

Venomous Snakes: Snakes in general are shy and
do not like to be
around humans,
though some
species are more
aggressive than
others. They'll

bite if they feel threatened, just like any other
wild animal, and so the best way to avoid a painful
bite is to keep away. Should you stumble upon a
snake, slowly move away.

Here's some good news: Snake bites do not
always deliver venom. This is because many
snakes can control release of their venom. The
bigger the perceived threat, the more dangerous
the bite. You may be lucky enough to simply
escape with puncture wounds, though in this case
you run the risk of tetanus, a bacterial infection.
Treat the bite as you would regular a puncture
wound.

If you or someone else gets bitten, and
there's a chance the bite did deliver venom, move
beyond striking distance of the snake. Note the

snake's appearance so that you can describe it to emergency staff. Have the person lie down, keeping the wound below the heart, so the venom doesn't spread readily. To slow the venom's spread even more, keep the person calm and at rest – keeping still is key. Cover the wound with a loose, sterile bandage. Remove shoes if the foot or leg was bitten; if the is in an area where there is jewelry, remove the jewelry.

DO NOT cut the wound – this does nothing to help stop the venom from spreading and increases risk of bacterial infection. DO NO attempt to suck the venom out. It will be absorbed into the mouth and spread through the body, putting the helper at risk. DO NOT apply ice, water, or a tourniquet. DO NOT give the person caffeinated drinks, alcohol, or any medications.

The most important rule about encountering wild animals is **KEEP YOUR DISTANCE**. You have likely heard many news reports about women, men, and children who were seriously injured or died during a close encounter with a wild animal. Someone you know may have a story about a relative who was hurt because they didn't back off soon enough or bothered an animal on purpose. Avoid becoming the next news story, and respect wild animals by giving them plenty of space and admiring them from a distance.

CHAPTER 4: What About Insects and Bugs?

Believe it or not, insects and bugs are a bigger danger than snakes or big animals. Every year more people die from insect bites and bug bites than from snakebites or bites from big animals. Read about what insects you are likely to meet where you're going, and in all cases, wearing repellent or clothes which have repellent in them is a smart idea. Wear sturdy boots to protect your feet, and keep your pant legs tucked into your socks to keep ticks and other biting insects at bay. Check your body regularly for any insects which may have hitched a ride, especially after moving through thick brush. Do not touch insects that you see and don't put your hand into random holes – insects will bite if they think you're trying to chase them out of their homes.

 If you ever are attacked by a swarm of wasps or bees, RUN! Keep your face and airways covered with a shirt, a bandanna, or something else. Bees are attracted to carbon dioxide, and when you're breathing you're breathing out a lot of it. They'll follow the trail the way a hunting dog will follow the trail of prey.

Find shelter as fast as you can, like a car or building that can be securely shut. If you're a long way from shelter, try to rush through brush or shrubs to distract the swarm. Otherwise just keep moving until the swarm gives up the chase. Once you're safe, check for any stingers and remove them as soon as possible. Get medical attention immediately if you or someone else shows signs of an allergic reaction, or even if you just have a lot of stings. Better safe than sorry. DO NOT attempt to escape by jumping into water. A swarm can linger over water for a while, long enough to still be there when you come up for air.

DO NOT spray a hose at someone who is being chased by bees. This will just make the bees angrier and more likely to keep up the chase. DO NOT stand still and swat at the bees or wasps. Quick movements will agitate them further.

Kissing Bugs: These nocturnal insects are called such because they tend to bite people's faces. While most people don't have much of a reaction beyond mild itching, swelling, and redness, occasionally a kissing bug bite can cause a severe allergic reaction. Seek medical attention immediately.

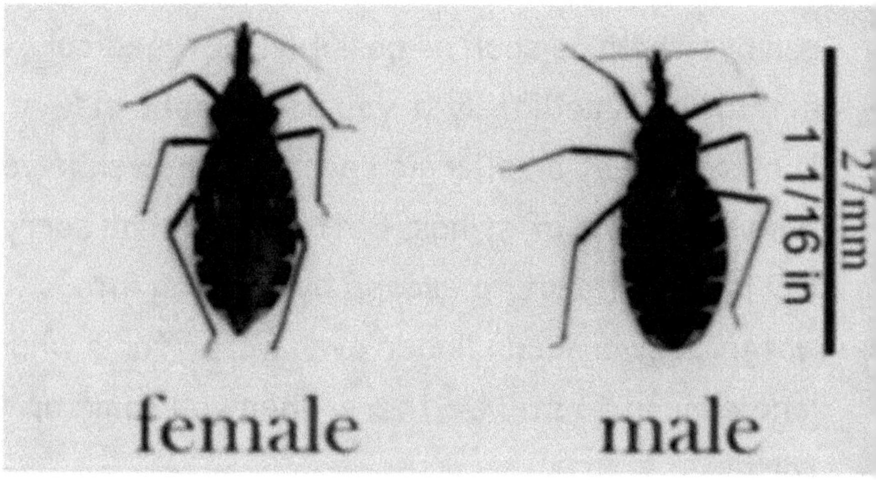

Another risk from a kissing bug bite is Chagas disease, which is caused by a parasite named *Trypanosoma cruzi*. This parasite lives in the kissing bug's feces and intestines. Thankfully, kissing bugs rarely transmit this parasite to humans. Really, the only time you get Chagas disease is if the feces from a kissing bug get into your body. (Listen to your parents and remember to wash your face in the morning). In the acute phase of Chagas, early symptoms can mimic a mild case of the flu; you may not know if you've contracted Chagas disease until later on, sometimes 10 to 25 years later. There's no cure for this disease once it reaches the chronic stage, where symptoms are life-threatening. So if you think you've been bitten by an infected kissing bug, seek medical treatment ASAP.

Mosquitoes: These are pretty much every human's least favorite insect because of their bloodsucking habits and the horrible itching welts they leave behind. Mosquitoes can be found all over the world so it's actually very hard to avoid them completely. The best you can do is take steps to reduce your chances of being bitten and thus being exposed to a variety of nasty diseases. Avoid going outside when mosquitoes are most active. As there are over 3,000 species of mosquitoes worldwide, this period of high activity can vary. You'll need to be aware of what species are commonly found where you are in order to determine when to avoid being outdoors.

However, sometimes you must be outside at the same time that mosquitoes are highly active. So make sure to wear insect repellent. Wear long pants and long-sleeved shirts, and if you can get clothing with repellent in it, so much the better. Wear a hat to protect your head from being bitten. Cover as much of your body as you can while remaining comfortable and make sure you will be able to move around without much trouble.

Avoid being around standing water, as mosquitoes lay their eggs in it. If you have fine netting, set it up so it forms a canopy over your sleeping spot and protects you from mosquitoes and other insects while you sleep. Proper mosquito nets have been dipped in an insecticide so that they repel and kill mosquitoes.

Ticks and Ants: Ordinary black ants are not usually a big concern for people. The most you have to worry about is whether they've gotten into your food supply. Fire ants and a few other species, though, present more of a problem. These ants deliver a nasty, painful bite, and if you're unlucky enough to be attacked by a swarm of them, it can end badly. Much like mosquitoes, ants can be found in many places in the world so avoiding them entirely is not possible.

The most you can do is keep your food securely stored so ants can't get into it and avoid disturbing any nests you may find when out and about. Check your bed and anywhere else you think ants could have gotten in. Since you can't avoid ants, you can at least reduce your chances of getting bitten.

Ticks have a horrible reputation for spreading disease. Feeding on blood as they do, these insects are exposed to all sorts of bacteria and parasites which can then be spread to a human host. They're very small and are very hard to see; for many people they only realize they have a tick attached to them after the tick has fed and increased in size. Again, wear repellent designed to keep ticks away (all the better if you find one that keeps away multiple species of biting insects). Keep your body covered as much as you can when outside. Check often to make sure a tick hasn't hitched a ride on you. Light-colored clothes make this an easier job, as ticks are easier to see than if you wore dark clothes.

If you do find a tick has latched onto you or someone else, you should remove it. Get a pair of pointy tweezers and have a container of soapy water or rubbing alcohol on hand. First, clean the area around the bite with rubbing alcohol. Get those tweezers right down on the skin – you must grab as close to the tick's head as you can. Once you've got the tick in your tweezers, pull up slow and firm. Don't twist or jerk because this can cause the tick's head to detach from its body and remain attached to the skin. Keep pulling straight up with steady pressure until the tick comes off. Clean the bite area with rubbing alcohol or soap and water, and your hands too.

As for the tick, most people just want it gone. Drowning it in rubbing alcohol or soapy water, wrapping it tightly in tape or a scrap of paper before throwing it out, are two options. At home people will sometimes flush the tick down the toilet, but that's not possible in the wild. DO NOT crush the tick with your bare fingers. You can get sick from it that way.

 As with other insects, you can't avoid spiders entirely

(unless you're in a polar region). There are so many species of spiders in the world that it's best to research which ones you're likely to encounter in a given area. In general, though, spiders avoid bothering humans and will not bite unless they feel threatened. You'll need to be extra cautious in a region where there are many dangerous spiders around. A bite from a non-venomous spider can hurt but treat it as you would any other insect bite. Get bitten by a brown recluse or another venomous spider, and you must act quickly.

Clean the site with soap and water. Apply a cool compress. If you think the bite came from a venomous spider, and the bite is on an arm, hand, foot, or other extremity, elevate it. You can slow or halt the venom's spread by tying a snug bandage above the bite, but don't tie it so tight that it cuts off circulation. Adults can take antihistamines or painkillers to relieve mild spider bite symptoms (use caution when giving these medications to teenagers and children). Severe spider bite symptoms or those which get worse for more than 24 hours require medical attention.

Scorpions are plenty scary-looking. Their sting is painful, but most stings won't need serious medical treatment. Severe symptoms, however, absolutely call for a trip to the nearest hospital.

The following are symptoms which may be present at the site of a scorpion sting:

-Pain, can be intense

-Slight swelling

-Numbness and tingling

-Warmth

Nothing too scary, right? If that's the worst to happen, then there's nothing to worry about. You need to seek medical attention as soon as possible should more severe symptoms begin. The following symptoms are related to widespread venom effects and usually occur in children who have been stung:

-Difficulty breathing

-Sweating

-Nausea and vomiting

-Drooling

-Muscle twitching or thrashing

-Unusual head, neck and eye movements

-High blood pressure (hypertension)

-Accelerated heart rate (tachycardia)

-Excitability or restlessness, or inconsolable crying

It is possible for someone to have an allergic reaction to a scorpion sting. Look for signs and symptoms similar to those of an allergic reaction to a bee sting. Get medical care immediately when these symptoms appear.

If you can't get to a hospital right away follow these steps to treat a scorpion sting and keep a person safe until they can see a doctor.

-Clean the wound with mild soap and water.

-Apply a cool compress. This may help reduce pain.

-Take a painkiller as needed. If the victim is a child, try giving them Children's Motrin or another approved painkiller.

-Don't eat or drink if you are having trouble swallowing. If someone else was stung and they are having trouble swallowing, don't let them have food or liquids.

There is the risk of getting tetanus, and you should check that you or the victim's vaccination records are up to date. Otherwise a tetanus shot may be given once the victim is better.

Leeches:

These bloodsucking critters are found all over the world. Most prefer to live in shallow bodies

of fresh water, and some can be found in oceans or in moist soil. If you find a leech attached to your body, don't panic. The majority of leech bites are not harmful. As with any bite, there's a risk of infection or an allergic reaction, but the latter is not a concern for most people.

On the downside, you don't know where this leech has been. You don't know what it has has fed from before latching onto you. So while you shouldn't panic, you should still be alert for signs that something is wrong. Leeches can carry parasites or viruses acquired from a previous host. Thankfully it is rare for these pathogens to be passed on to a human.

In the meantime, how do you remove a leech from your body? First, check to see how many there are – where there is one leech, it is possible to find more. You can wait for the leeches to finish feeding, at which point they'll fall off on their own. It can take from 30 minutes to an hour for a leech to get its fill of blood. If that doesn't suit you, it is time for immediate removal.

Check to see what part of your body the leech has latched onto. Check that none have somehow found their way into your nose or ears, if you were underwater. Those will be tricky, if not impossible to remove on your own!

Once you've figured out where the first leech and its friends are, locate the head. That would be the narrow end of a leech. The broad end is the sucker it uses to secure itself in place on a host.

Don't just grab the leech and pull. The mouthparts may stay in place and cause an infection. You need to detach the whole head. Place your fingernail (or any flat and rigid tool, like a nail file or plastic card) beside the head and slide it underneath until the head is completely separated from your skin.

The leech will attempt to attach itself to you again as soon as possible, so flick it off. Make sure to dispose of it as far away from any part of your, or from anyone in your group, as possible and as quickly as you can. Use an object to flick it away, since the leech might try to attach to your finger or hand.

Clean the wound. Because leech saliva contains an anticoagulant (prevents clotting) to help the leech get a steady flow of blood when feeding, the wound will bleed for a while. Left untreated, the wound can become infected and cause more serious problems later on. Wash the wound with soap and water. Dry with a clean cloth or paper towel. You can alcohol or iodine to sanitize the wound and the surrounding area before applying a clean dressing. Remember, the wound will keep on bleeding for a while, so you will need to change the bandage multiple times in a day. Seek medical help if the wound bleeds for more than a couple of days.

NOTE: Some people will suggest that you try to entice a leech to detach itself by putting shampoo or salt on it. Some will say you should try prodding it with a small flame or a burning stick. While any of these methods can cause a leech to to detach itself from you, the leech may also empty the contents of its stomach into the wound. Gross! We said above that leeches can carry parasites and other pathogens. If a leech throws up into a wound, this increases your chances of getting an infection or worse. If you want to remove a leech before it's done feeding, do it the right way.

CHAPTER 5: Finding Water and Building a Fire

How to locate Water

Water is perhaps the most important thing you need to find when out in the wild. Human bodies are made of mostly water and you need a clean, reliable supply to stay healthy. When trying to find water, watch for places where animal tracks meet. This can mean there's a water source nearby.

You can also look for bees and flies as a hint to where water can be. Bees won't fly very far from their nests in search of water. Watch to see which direction they fly in upon leaving the nest. Flies will stay even closer to water than bees.

Check to see where green vegetation is growing, such ferns and mosses. Even trees can be of help, though some will grow closer to water sources than others. Groundwater, which swells up from below the surface of the ground, can be found in various locations, but it requires you to dig to find it.

Water Purification

To purify water, you can boil it. This is a pretty common method. The water will taste flat, but you can fix that by pouring it back and forth between two pots or other containers a few times (the magic of aeration!). You can use iodine tablets or another packaged form of water purifier. Follow the manufacturer's directions.

NOTE: Rain and dew can also be gathered for drinking. Water from freshwater sources like lakes and streams must be purified before drinking to avoid waterborne illness. Boiling is an easy way to do this, and it requires the next thing we are going to talk about: fire.

Fire starters and fire-starting materials

Fire provides heat for warmth and cooking, and light. It's also great for keeping animals away as they know fire can hurt them. But first you need to prepare an area for the fire.

You can dig a shallow pit, or mark out a circle with rocks. If it's very windy, you can try building a wall on one side of the fire area with rocks or some other debris to block the wind. Make sure your fire area is neither too close or too far from a steady supply of fuel. If necessary, gather extra wood or chop some and pile it in a safe spot in your camp. If possible, cover your fuel supply with tarp or something else to protect it from rain and snow. Wet wood doesn't burn properly, just makes lots of smoke if it burns at all.

Once you've got your fire area set up, grab some tinder, some small pieces of wood, and some larger pieces. It's time to build your fire!

There are several ways you can go about building a fire.

1) **Matches.** Ideally you should always keep a small container of these in your survival kit. Waterproof ones are preferable to regular ones,

and if you can, get matches that are made of sustainably harvested wood rather than cardboard as they are stronger and won't bend easily. You can make matches waterproof by dipping the head in wax and leaving them to dry. When you need to use them, simply scrape the protective coating of wax off and you'll have a nice dry match to work with.

2) **Flint & steel**. Many years ago, before matches were invented, people would carry a piece of

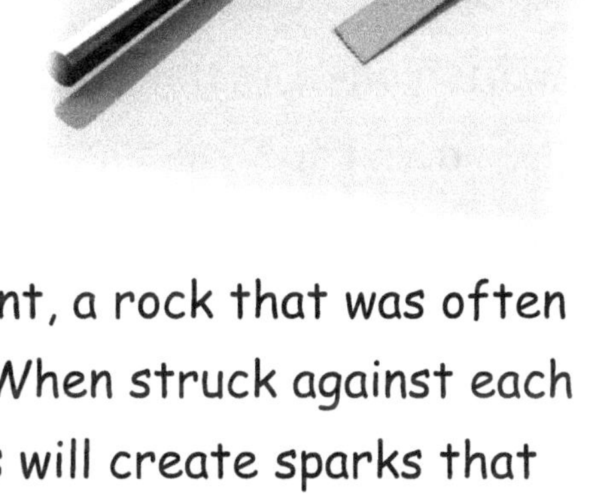

steel and a piece of flint, a rock that was often used for fire-making. When struck against each other, these two items will create sparks that can ignite a piece of lint, dry grass, or some other flammable material, which you can use to make a fire. In a pinch, you can use the blade of a pocketknife as the steel.

3) **Magnifying glass or eyeglasses**. The trick here is to hold the lens at just the right angle to focus sunlight into a small area. Do that, and soon enough your tinder with be on fire. But you do need plenty of sunlight for this method to work – if the day is overcast or it's nighttime, you'll have to try something else.

4) **Hand drill or bow drill**. Both of these use frictions to create heat and start a fire. The main difference is that the latter uses a sort of bow fashioned from a flexible piece of wood and a shoelace, rope, or something that won't break under so much friction. You'll also need a socket (which can be a rock or another, smaller piece of wood) to put pressure on the end of the spindle that you hold while you're rotating it with the bow.

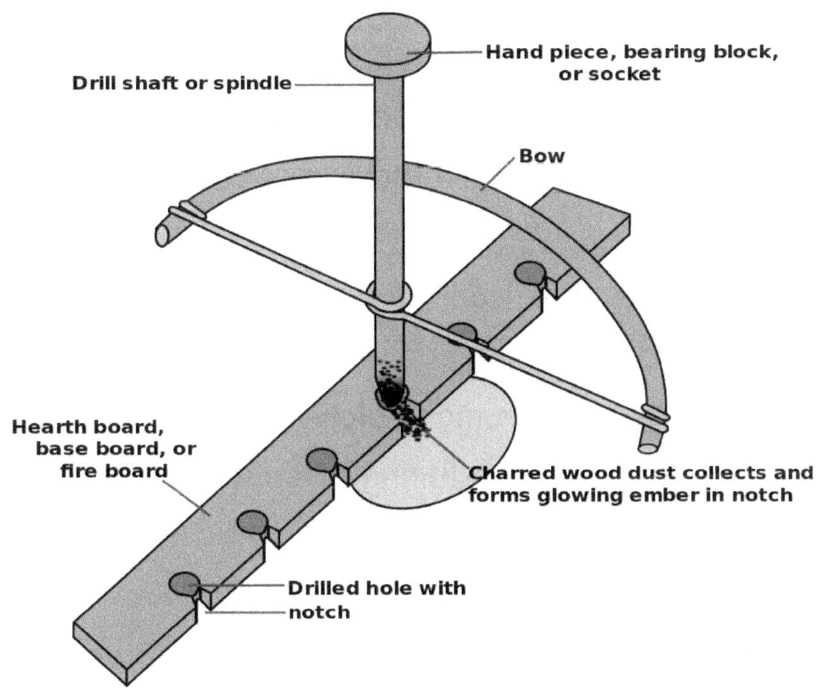

Get a flat piece of wood, cut a v-shaped notch
and a create a depression next to that. Place
your tinder under the notch. Catch your spindle
in a loop of the bowstring and place one end in
the fireboard. Putting pressure on the other end,
start sawing. It will probably take some time
before you see an ember glowing. When you do,
drop that ember into the tinder and gently blow
on it. Presto, fire!

FUEL: While any dry wood will burn, different types of wood have different properties that will make them more suitable for certain purposes.

First, know that wood is divided into two types: hardwood and softwood. Most hardwoods are dense and so burn more slowly. They are great for cooking and producing fires which burn hot and intense – perfect for warming the inside of a house or cabin. Softwoods, on the other hand, are not as dense. They ignite faster and emit more smoke than hardwoods, so it is best to burn these outside.

OAK: One of the most common types of hardwood. Best used for fires that you need to have burning for a long time. In some cases you may want to use it in a mix of different types of wood.

BLACK CHERRY: Easy to handle and easy to split. This hardwood gives off little smoke and a moderate number of sparks. It also produces a solid amount of heat so it is a good choice for summer or spring camping. There's also it's delightful aroma, which adds a nice flavor to any foods cooked or smoked over it.

ASH: This hardwood is a favorite because it burns quite well on its own (medium to hot range), produces a steady flame and has a great heat output. Would be a fine choice to burn in a chimney or wood-burning stove. White ash is your best bet.

BEECH: Another hardwood that burns long and hot, and that makes it an optimal choice for cold weather camping and survival. It emits an enormous amount of heat with few sparks and little smoke.

BIRCH: This softwood burns quickly and well. There are many species of birch and they all burn with varying degrees of efficiency. The bark can also be used as a natural fire starter. You can try burning it with oak if you want to have a fire that will last through the night is needed.

DOGWOOD: Compact and heavy hardwood, which makes it a great choice for firewood. It emits a small amount of smoke and sparks, and produces a bold flame. That being said, the dogwood tree is ornamental, and the base of its trunk smaller, so you are better off using this for quick camping trips.

FIR: This softwood should, ideally, be left to season for a year before being used. Out in the wild, you likely haven't got that time, but even unseasoned fir will produce medium to hot flames. It smells wonderful too.

MAPLE: Like oak, this hardwood is dense and a bit hard to chop. It burns for a long time, though, and the flames it produces are very powerful. Maple produces a lot of heat with only a small amount of smoke. If you're wondering, of the several types of maple, the best ones to use for sustaining a long fire are silver, sugar, Manitoba, and red maple.

CEDAR: Another softwood commonly encountered in the woods. Cedar gives off a pleasant smell when burned. It will give a lasting heat with little flame, though there will be some crackling due to the sap. You may want to stick with burning smaller pieces, though.

ELM: There are two species: red elm and white, or American elm. Both are hardwoods. Red elm makes for good firewood. While it doesn't burn as hot as some other woods, its heat output is good. It's a bit stringy, but will split nicely. White elm doesn't burn very hot and is tough to split. Lots of people don't like it for that reason. The wood is stringy and can hold a lot of moisture, making it unsuitable for use unless seasoned.

PINE: A softwood that lights easily and burns fast with a good flame. You will need to refuel more often, however, if you use it. With its high sap and resin content, pine is best burned outdoors. Works great as a firestarter.

LARCH: This is the hardest of all softwoods, and it is actually harder than some hardwoods. It will burn very hot, but it gives off a lot of smoke so you had better burn it outdoors or have the door of your shelter open to let the smoke out. You can mix it with hardwoods for a fire that will burn hot and last long.

TAMARACK: This softwood needs to season before it's properly ready for a fire, but it is on the dense side. Tamarack burns as steadily and as hot as a hardwood.

APPLE: It's a fruit tree, so when you burn it, it produces a lovely scent. Burns steadily.

WALNUT: Another hardwood, beloved by those who used wood-burning stoves. A slow and steady-burning wood, it doesn't produce much smoke.

HICKORY: This is one of the densest hardwoods, difficult to split. It burns quite well, though, and is a popular choice for grilling or smoking foods.

BLACK LOCUST: This tree species isn't very abundant or well-known, but it makes great firewood. The wood is strong and dense, and is famous for making fence posts.

Those are just a few of the woods you can choose from to fuel your fire. But there are also woods which you should avoid burning, even outside. You'll notice that we mentioned some woods must season, or dry out, before burning. That is because these woods, when freshly cut, have lots of sap and a high moisture content. It is thus not easy to light, nor is it easy to keep a fire made with greenwood lit. Greenwood also produces far too much smoke, and if you use it in your wood-burning stove or fireplace, it will leave deposits on the cooler parts – you might find yourself using some very coarse words during the very unpleasant cleanup.

DRIFTWOOD: Despite the stories you hear about beautiful fires made with driftwood, remember that those are normally built in the open air. Driftwood contains a lot of salt, and when burned, it releases dioxin. This chemical is a known carcinogenic (cancer-causing substance). Never burn driftwood indoors, and exercise caution even if you burn it outdoors.

ANYTHING WITH "POISON" IN THE NAME: No explanation needed. Really, stay away and find something else to burn.

ENDANGERED SPECIES: Besides the 12 or threatened or endangered species of tree in North America, there are species worldwide that have been put on that list. Try to avoid using any of them in your fire, never mind for building a shelter.

MEXICAN ELDER: This fast-growing, semi-evergreen tree is found in the southern USA and is a natural source of cyanide. Even inhaling smoke from a burning piece of it can cause cyanide poisoning.

HEMLOCK: Not to be confused with the poisonous plant which shares its name. The problem with hemlock is that it is full of extremely hard knots which makes it very difficult to split the trees into burnable logs. It also produces a lot of sparks, not something you want in a firewood, whether you burn it outside or inside.

ASPEN, WILLOW, BASSWOOD: Softwoods of very poor quality for burning and producing heat.

OLEANDER: Every part of this tree is toxic. Don't even use a branch to toast marshmallows or bake campfire bread.

PAINTED, STAINED, OR TREATED WOOD: Humans live almost everywhere, and with us, come things like wood that's got paint, varnish, or other chemicals on it and in it. If you come across any such wood when out in the wild, do not use it for fuel. You can use it build part of a shelter, but burning it is not safe, even outdoors.

CHAPTER 6: Signaling for Help

In a survival situation, it helps to know how to signal for help. You have a few options, but which ones you can use will depend on what you have available, the weather, your location, and other factors.

Emergency Flares: **If you've ever seen someone set off a type of firework called a Roman candle, then you have an idea of how these works. Unlike with the firework, the pieces that is launched high into the air stays lit for longer so that people can see 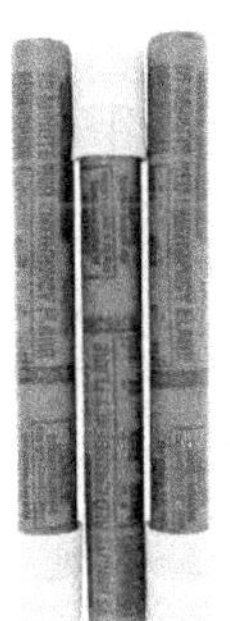 it. These are great to use in large clearings, or on mountainsides, any place where there are not a lot of trees hiding you from sight. Some flares are handheld, though these can be harder for rescue workers to see.**

Smoke Signals: These were used by many Indigenous tribes to communicate with others from afar. Just building a fire and adding wet leaves or other materials that send up thick smoke will be enough to alert people that something is going on. There is a method for using a fire and a wet blanket or perhaps a tarp, to send clouds of smoke into the air in patterns meant to signal distress. Useful, but this takes some practice to get right. Smoke signals work great in spots that aren't too far from a fuel source, but have enough clearance around them that the smoke will not be hidden from sight.

ONE SMOKE PUFF: Commonly used as an attention signal. Something is going on but there's no imminent danger or cause for alarm.

TWO SMOKE PUFFS: All is well.

THREE SMOKE PUFFS: This is the one you want

to send when you're trying to tell others you're in danger or that there is an emergency.

Mirror: Sunlight can be reflected off a mirror and directed at the sky, or at a rescue helicopter if you see one coming. Your best chance of getting someone's attention is to try and get the flash of sunlight into their eyes. Naturally people will want to try and find the reason why they were just temporarily blinded. Keep flashing the mirror until it's clear you've been seen. If the sky is cloudy, or it's nighttime, you best think of another way to signal for help.

Survival Emergency Whistle: This is one of the best-known methods, though it works best if you already know people are nearby. An emergency whistle should be part of everyone's survival kit, and the one you're probably most familiar with is bright orange in color with a carrying cord attached. It may even have a compass attached. Others are made of metal. Some come with flashlights built int! There are a variety of choices on the market and it is really up to you to decide which one(s) best suit your needs.

Some are the classic whistle with a pea, a tiny ball of metal or plastic, placed inside to create a shrill noise; others don't have that pea. A whistle with a pea is the most common type, and so will be more affordable to buy. The downside is that these whistles aren't very hygienic and the pea can sometimes jam if it gets wet from too much saliva or from rain. Peals whistles don't have the last problem, but they do require more cleaning and they are more expensive.

Lose your whistle? Forget to pack it? Did it break? Improvise with anything that, when blown into, makes a loud shrill noise. Just make sure that you will not hurt yourself by using whatever you happen to find (splinters, cutting your mouth on rusty metal, etc.). It may not be as loud as a proper whistle, but in an emergency you have to make do with whatever you have.

To signal for help with your whistles, there are two common methods.

Method 1: Use your whistle to blast out the classic SOS pattern: three short whistles, then three long ones, followed by another three short whistles. Pause for breath and then repeat the pattern. Do this for as long as you can – it's the best way to increase your chances of being found.

Method 2: 3-Blast Signal – All you need to do is blow three loud, short blasts on your whistle. Count in your head to three as you blow so that each blast lasts about three seconds. Pause to take a breath and give the sound time to travel, then repeat. Do this for as long as you can to give yourself the best chance of being found.

CHAPTER 7: Dealing with Extreme Weather

One of the worst parts about being in a survival situation is dealing with extreme weather. Humans, even with all our knowledge and advanced technology, are still very much at the mercy of the weather. If we're not careful and aware, we leave ourselves vulnerable to illness, injury or even death.

The most important thing to do in extreme weather events is find to safe shelter. No time for building a lean-to or pitching a tent – you must find a safe place as soon as possible. Depending on what type of event, this can range from finding high ground to avoiding flooding, a cave to hide from wind and rain, or anything that will let you wait in relative safety and comfort until it's safe to venture outside.

Aside from weather events, we must also understand that just being outside when it's very cold or hot leaves us vulnerable to all sorts of dangers.

Hypothermia: This occurs when the body loses heat faster than it can produce it, resulting in a dangerously low body temperature. It can be due to being out in the cold too long, not being dressed warmly enough, or being immersed in cold water – anything that exposes you to the cold for a longer period of time. If your body temperature starts to fall below 95°F (35°C), you're entering the danger zone.

Signs of hypothermia include shivering, weak pulse, slow and shallow breathing, slurred speech or mumbling, confusion, low energy level or drowsiness, clumsiness, and even loss of consciousness. With infants, you may also see bright read skin that is cold to the touch. Because these symptoms often begin gradually, the victim doesn't know what is happening; confused thinking interferes with self-awareness and can lead to risky-taking behavior.

This is a serious situation that usually would require getting medical attention. If you're stranded out in the wild, though, the most you can do is provide first aid. Get the person out of the cold and into a safe, warm spot. Be gentle – they likely do not understand what is happening, and excessive, vigorous or jarring movement can trigger cardiac arrest. Limit movement to only what is necessary.

If the person's clothes are wet, remove those. Cover the person with blankets, quilts, or coats to warm them. Be mindful of the person's head – you must insulate it from the cold, especially if you are outside where the ground is very cold. Cover the person's head so that only their face is showing.

Monitor their breathing. Perform CPR if you're trained in it and the person's breathing is dangerously low or has stopped.

The name of the game is to keep the person warm and comfortable. Besides covering them, provide warm beverages, as long as they are alert and able to swallow. Stay away from caffeine and alcohol. Sweet beverages will provide not only warmth but a bit of quick energy. Use warm, dry compresses on the neck, chest, and groin only. DO NOT apply direct in the form of hot water, or a heating pad or lamp. This can damage the skin or cause irregular heartbeats so severe that the heart stops.

Frostbite: Frostbite occurs when a body part has been exposed to cold for so long that blood flow begins to slow and eventually stop. Exposed skin turns red or may get sore. This is actually the early stage of frostbite, called "frostnip."

There are three stages of frostbite. Early frostbite only affects the top layers of skin. More advanced cases can go all the way down to muscle and bone.

Early stage: The skin turns a pale yellow or white.
The person may feel a burning sensation, or
itching, stinging, or the classic "pins and needles."

Intermediate stage: Skin has hardened. It also
looks waxy or shiny. If, at this stage, you spot
the problem and treat it, blisters filled with fluid
or blood will form.

Advanced stage: The worst case scenario is when
the skin of the affected area feels hard and cold
to the touch. It will darken quickly and begins to
turn black – a sign of irreparable damage. An
affected limb may even fall off or have to be
amputated. At that stage there is little you can
do. If, however, you become aware of the
problem well before then, you can treat
frostbite easily enough.

Do not rub the affected area. If you've caught it
early and the frostbite is in a hand, foot, or some
other extremity, you can hold the body part
under your armpit to warm it. You can soak the

affected area in warm water (no more than 104 to 107 degrees F). If the frostbite is in an area that can't be submerged, place a warm, wet washcloth on it. Keep the cloth there for at least 30 minutes. You can cover frostbitten ears with yours hands, and so the same for noses, as long as it is the early stage. If there is more than one person present, you can take turns warming the victim's frostbitten body part.

Heat Illness: Any disorder which is due to exposure to heat is considered heat illness.

-Heat cramps: Muscle pains which happen during heavy exercise in hot weather. Not usually serious but can be a sign of something worse. To avoid these, stay hydrated and eat potassium-rich foods. To treat heat cramps, avoid hard work and exercise for several hours so the body can recover.

-Heatstroke: This is defined by a body temperature of more than 104°F (40°C) due to lack of proper thermoregulation with heat exposure. Dry skin, rapid, strong pulse and dizziness are some of the symptoms. A person with heatstroke must have their body temperature lowered quickly. Move them to a cool or at least shady spot and remove their clothing to promote heat loss. You can also bath them in cold water or put cold compression the neck, head, torso, and groin to further help cool the victim. Immersing them in cold water is another method, but you may need the help of several people to do it. It should be avoided for an unconscious person, but if there's no other option, the person's head must be held above water.

Whatever you do, monitor the person's breathing and heart rate. If the person is conscious and can swallow, you can try giving them small amounts of water or a sports drink to help them re-hydrate. Don't overdo it – drinking too much liquid, even water, can be just as

dangerous as dehydration. Get medical attention
as soon as you can.

-Heat edema (swelling: Can occur in the legs,
hands, or other body parts. In the case of legs
and hands, it can occur when you've sat or stood
in a hot environment for a long time. Heat causes
temporary dilation of the blood vessels, and fluid
can pool in legs and feet, or elsewhere. A sure
sign you have edema is when an indentation
remains after you press a finger into your
swollen skin for several seconds.

Certain medical conditions can leave a
person more susceptible developing edema. Older
people, pregnant women, and overweight people
are also prone to this condition. But even young,
healthy pepole can be at risk if there is limited
access to air-conditioning, or if they perform
high-intensity workouts outside in high heat.

Mild edema can be treated by elevating the
legs and feet, or even the hands. Brief walking

and simple leg movements can help ease the swelling.

To prevent heat edema, avoid extreme heat as much as possible. Drink plenty of fluids to prevent dehydration. Keeping the body cool can minimize dilation of blood vessels and keep fluid from pooling in limbs. If you must be outdoors in high heat, take a lot of breaks to cool down. Gradually acclimate yourself to the weather (get used to it). Avoid prolonged sitting or standing as much as possible.

-Heat syncope: Dizziness or faintness caused by overheating. The basic symptom is fainting, with or without mental confusions. It is caused by peripheral blood vessel dilation, which leads to diminished blood flow to the brain and dehydration.

Other symptoms include:
-Headache
-Nausea

-Vomiting

-Increased pulse

As with all heat illness, the best prevention is to avoid strenuous physical activity in hot weather. Avoid alcohol in hot weather because it causes dehydration, which can make symptoms worse. If you must engage in physical activities during hot weather, drink plenty of water even a sports drink to make sure you are getting enough fluid and electrolytes.

Anyone who starts to show symptoms of heat syncope should be moved to a shaded or cool area. Have them sit down, or lie in their back, with their legs raised. Water containing a little salt, or some other drink with electrolytes, should be given in slowly, in small amounts. Make sure they rest and recover, because heat syncope can lead to heat exhaustion or heatstroke.

-Heat exhaustion: Can be a precursor to heatstroke. It's caused by losing water and electrolytes through sweating faster than a person can replace these things. Symptoms include vomiting, dizziness, nausea, excessive sweating, irritability, weakness, thirst, high body temperature, headache, and decreased urination (peeing).

First aid for heat exhaustion involves moving the person to a cool place and removing extra layers of clothes to cool them down. You can fan them or put wet towels on them. If they are dizzy, have them lie down and prop their feet up. If they are conscious and aware, have them drink water or a sports drink to replace lost fluids. Don't do this if they are too confused, vomiting, or unconscious. Also, if they are vomiting, turn the person on their side so they don't choke. Get them to a doctor as soon as possible.

-Heat tetany: Not as talked about as the previous disorders but it's no less serious. It usually results from short periods of stress in intense heat. Symptoms can include numbness or tingling, muscle spasms, respiratory problems, and hyperventilation. Treatment included getting the affected person away from heat and lowering the breathing rate. Heat tetany can also be a symptom of a more serious problem.

Sun or Snow Blindness: This happens due to overexposing the eyes to UV light, especially without protection. It's very common among skiers, who must deal with the sunlight reflecting off snow, and people who spend a lot of time on the water, as the sunlight reflects off the surface quite readily. It affects the cornea (that transparent outer layer of your eye) and is basically the equivalent of a sunburn

Symptoms of sun or snow blindness don't always appear right away. Sometimes it takes several hours for them to show. They include:

-feeling that something is in your eye and you can't remove it

-pain and burning in your eyes

-swollen, red eyelids

-watery eyes

-headache

-blurred vision

-exaggerated glare around indoor lights

Less common: temporary vision loss and temporary color changes in vision

There's not much you can do to treat sun or snow blindness aside from resting your eyes away from UV light. If you wear contacts, remove them immediately and don't put them in until your eyes have healed. You can try using a cold compress to soothe any pain, and taking painkillers is an option if the compress doesn't help much. Using artificial tears to keep the eyes moisturized will help them heal. Sun and snow blindness go away once the corneas recover, with symptoms resolving over a day or two.

To prevent snow or sun blindness, wear sunglasses which block 100 percent of the sun's

UV rays. Check that the lenses are dark enough to make going out in the sun comfortable, but light enough for you to see where you are going. This is where interchangeable lenses come in handy. If you are in an area where there's snow, wear sunglasses with a close-fitting, war-around style frame, or snow goggles. Be aware that UV radiation penetrates clouds, so you can get sunburned eyes even on overcast or cloudy days.

Assessing the weather

The best way to figure out what kind of weather is in store is to check the weather forecast. When you are out in the wilderness, though, sometimes you can't get service on your cell phone and you may not have brought a satellite phone. Well, now what do you do if you want to see if the weather is about to change? Look at the sky

Clouds, for example, can tell you a lot about what weather to expect if you know what to look for. The higher the clouds are, the better and more stable the weather is likely to be. Generally, storm clouds are dark-colored or even black, low, and massed in large clusters. Very low clouds can cover high ground with mist or fog. Fair-weather clouds tend to be high and white

See below for some cloud types and what they mean.

CUMLUS: These fluffy clouds usually indicate good weather. If they are dark in color and clustered  together, however, that's a possible sign of rain. When they are seen floating over the open ocean, cumulus clouds can indicate that land is nearby.

CIRRUS: These white, wispy clouds tend to form at very high altitudes in good weather. Because

the air at those heights is so cold, cirrus clouds
are made entirely from crystals of ice! They are
sometimes called
"mare's tails."

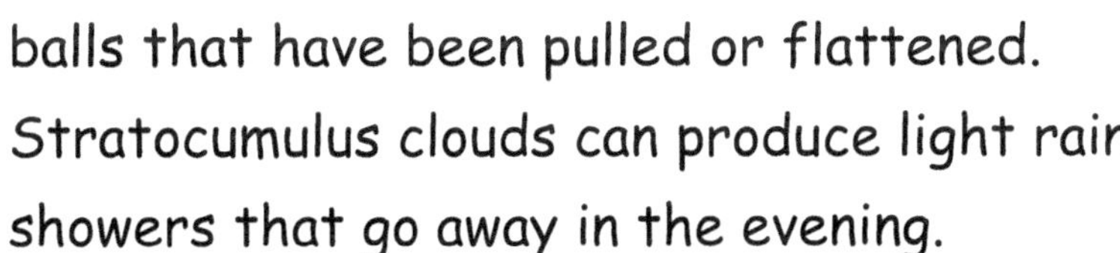

STRATOCUMULUS:
These will sometimes
form on top of cumulus
clouds. You will see
them spreading out in a
thick sheet, and they
look almost like cotton
balls that have been pulled or flattened.
Stratocumulus clouds can produce light rain
showers that go away in the evening.

There are other ways to predict what the weather maybe like. For example, morning mist or fog can indicate stable weather. A clear sky at night means a cold, possibly frosty, night since there are no clouds to retain heat. If you or someone in your group feels pain at the site of an old injury or in your joints, it can mean rain is coming. Pine cones react to humidity, so check around you to see if there are any lying around. When the air is dry, the scales on a pine cone will shrivel and cone opens up. Just before wet weather comes, the scale absorb moisture from the air and the cone regains its natural shape.

CHAPTER 8: Finding Food

Plants (and Animals) to avoid and Edible ones

Finding food takes patience, a sharp eye, and some knowledge of what is safe to eat and what isn't. You can observe the local wildlife to see what they eat. Lots of foods that animals eat are safe for humans, but there are others which we can't eat.

Avoid plants that have stingers, have milky sap, or just any that you can't identify at all. If you do not know what it is, leave it alone and look for something more familiar to you.

Examples of poisonous plants: mountain laurel, poison ivy, cedar trees (they may smell nice, but no part of them is safe to eat), Death camas/death lily, daffodil, cowbane, deadly nightshade, baneberry, to name a few.

Don't worry, there are many plants which are safe to eat. Examples of edible plants and plant parts:

Cattails (roots)

Blueberries

Raspberries

Roses (rose hips, high in Vitamin C)

Wild cherries (though choke cherries are particularly bitter-tasting)

Wild strawberries

Wintergreen berries (can also make a tea using the leaves)

Blackberries

Pickerelweed (nutlets)

Arrowhead (tubers make a good potato substitute)

Sweet fern (leaves for tea, edible nutlets)

Pine needles (tea), pine tree seeds

Dandelion (every part – roots should be boiled in salted water)

Clover (roots, flower, leaves are good raw or cooked)

Acorns

Brazil nuts

Coconuts and young coconut shoots

Spruce needles (boil to make tea)

Inner bark of the birch tree (eat raw or boiled; birch sap is drinkable)

Prickly pear (fruit)

Saguaro cactus (fruit)

Yucca (eat flowers raw or cooked: fruit must be boiled, peeled and de-seeded)

Date palm fruit

Grasses (eat young shoots, steams, and leaves cooked or raw)

Carob

Tamarind

Aspen (inner bark)

Jerusalem artichoke (yes, this grows wild – tubers are edible)

Water lily (seeds, tuber, and stem)

Cloudberries

Carrageen seaweed (eat fresh, dried, or cooked into a sort of pudding)

Laver (leaves eaten boiled)

NOTE: Unless you know your mushrooms very well, avoid eating any you find in the wild. Many people have died because they mistook a poisonous mushroom for an edible one. Lichen, on the other hand, are edible; there are no poisonous lichen in the world, but they all must be soaked in water overnight and then boiled well before eating.

If you find that you must take a chance on an unknown plant, give it the following taste test:

1) Crush a leaf. If it smells bad, or like almonds, discard it.

2) Rub the juice on the inside of your arm. If no irritation develops, place a small piece of the leaf on your lips for five seconds. Do the same for the corner of your mouth, on the tip of your tongue, and lastly under your tongue. Remember, each area should only have fives seconds of contact with the leaf.

4) If there is no stinging, swallow a small amount and wait for five hours. Eat nothing else during this time.

5) If you have no unpleasant reactions, the plant is safe to eat.

Or at least you can eat whatever part of the plant you have tested. All the same, play it safe and cook the plant. Also, be cautious when eating a plant that has been prepared differently than you are used to. Sometimes one cooking method is better at destroying chemicals which cause a reaction compared to another.

NOTE: Bamboo is a plant that is wonderful for multiple purpose, including as a food source. The shoots are the only edible part, but they must be thoroughly cooked to neutralize any chemicals which may make you sick. It also gets rid of any bitterness. The woody part of bamboo can be cut up to make a shelter. A section of bamboo with holes punched through each section except the bottom makes a good cooking pot: Pour enough water into the bamboo so that it doesn't quite reach the top. Lean this piece of bamboo over a fire with the open end propped up in a forked stick. As the water in the steam heats up, the steam which forms will cook any food placed in the top section. Bamboo can also be used to make light but very strong bow and arrows that you can use to hunt.

Need to build a raft? Make it out of
bamboo. Turn a piece of bamboo into a fishing
rod if don't have one or the one you brought
breaks. Need to store flour or dried meat or
fish? Take some bamboo and fashion storage
containers out of it. Bamboo sections can also be
used to transport water.

You can fashion a fishing spear from
bamboo. Make a drinking cup from a piece of
bamboo, but be careful – bamboo splinters easily
and it's not fun getting splinters in your mouth or
lips. You can even use it to make traps: place

pieces of bamboo inside a pit, or make a figure-4 deadfall trap to catch small prey. See below for directions on how to make this trap.

Step 1: Cut three sections of bamboo. Make notches so that the pieces will fit together to make a sort of frame. Cut the tips so they are angled.

Step 2: Find something heavy, something at least three times the weight of whatever animals you wish to trap. A large stone or log with a flat bottom is ideal.

Step 3: Find a good spot to place your trap. Make it a spot well away from where your campsite is so that your scent doesn't scare away small animals.

Step 4: Set one stick upright to act as the main support. Set another stick horizontally so that the pointed tip points toward the heavy weight (this will hold the bait). Set your trigger/release stick in place.

Step 5: Add the bait and leave the trap.

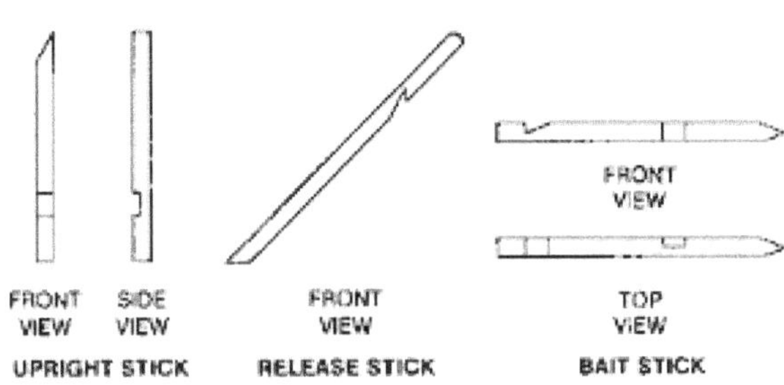

Come back in a while to see if you've

caught anything. If not, reset the trap and try again. You might want o even set more than one trap to increases your chances of success. Figure-4 traps are easy enough to build, but the trick is in getting them setup just right. The weight can't be too light nor can it be too heavy for the sticks to support. The trigger stick has to be set just right so that it will move in time for the weight to trap your prey. These are details that you will need to figure out over time.

CHAPTER 9: Learning to Navigate

Finding your way around is easy if you have a GPS-enabled device. But what if it breaks or runs out of power? That's when it's good to know how to navigate without relying on satellite technology.

Choosing a Map

People rely heavily on smartphones and other bits of technology to navigate. But in case your usual electronic navigator breaks, gets lost, or wont' work properly, you do have a backup option: a paper map.

These
maps seem old-
fashioned by
today's
standards, but a
good map paired
with a compass
can still help

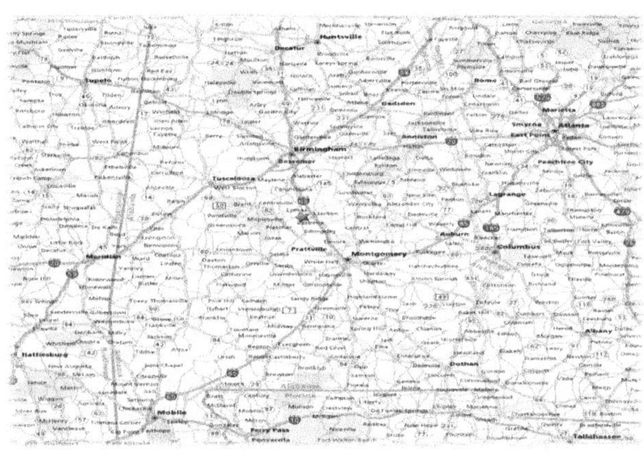

you find your way. There's more than one type of
map, so it's important to pick one that suits your
needs. If you're venturing into unfamiliar terrain,
you want a map that shows the whole area you
intend to visit.

A good map will have evenly-spaced grid
lines and a compass rose, which shows which way
is north, south, east, and west. The grid lines will
correspond to units of longitude and latitude. But
no matter how careful people are, sometimes you
get a map with some inaccuracies. It happens,
you're just going to have to allow for it.

There are different types of maps for
different purposes. Some are listed below.

ROAD MAPS: These are to help drivers navigate back roads and interstate highways. They tend to be very detailed, though the ones made for an entire country are less so, Road maps are usually made individually, according to the layout of a city or town.

TOPOGRAPHICAL MAPS: These show camper and hikers how to reach campsites and other lodging areas. Differences in elevation (how high up you are) and landscape will be shown with contour lines.

TOURIST MAPS: These highlight famous locations and landmarks for sightseers.

You may want to bring more than one map with you if you think you will be traveling through more than one area.

Compass: **One of the most important tools you can carry with you. Some emergency whistles will have one, which can be a backup in case your regular compass breaks or gets lost. A compass works via magnetism. The needle is magnetized such that one end will always point magnetic north and the other magnetic south, the poles of Earth's natural magnetic field. The only problem is that if you enter an area known for messing with a compass' magnetism, it will be useless at helping you find your way out. So we'll cover a few other ways to navigate.**

Using the Sun: **Before the earliest compasses were invented, humans would rely on the rising** and setting of the sun to find their way around. Sundials were used to tell what time of day it was, again relying on the sun's journey across the sky to keep track. If you have a watch, you can use it to orient yourself in relation to the sun. In the northern hemisphere, point the hour hand at the sun. Imagine a line halfway between the hour and 12 o'clock. At the head of that line will be south. In the southern hemisphere, you want to point the 12 o'clock mark at the sun. North lies halfway that mark and the hour hand.

Using the Stars: The stars are a fine way to navigate at night. Note that they don't actually move – they only appear to move thanks to the movement of the Earth on its axis. The only star which appears to not move is the North Star. In the northern hemisphere, this star can be used to find north. In the southern hemisphere, it's the Southern Cross that will help you find south.

Other: Use the environment around you to navigate. Plants grow towards the sun – facing south in the northern hemisphere and facing north in the southern hemisphere. Some species of birds can be used as basic direction finders. For example, several species of weaver builder their nests only the west sides of trees.

CHAPTER 10: What to Do If You or Someone Else is Injured

It's one of the scariest parts about being in the wilderness: You or someone else slips and falls, is attacked by an animal, or has an accident with their knife or some other tool. There's no emergency room, no 24-hour clinic or other place to get help. What do you do?

First, you must know what happened. Knowing what caused the injury is key to determining how to treat it. Ask the person what they were doing at the time they got hurt. If they are confused or otherwise unable to speak clearly, and there is someone else present, ask if they saw what happened.

Second, check the injury site. Is there heavy bleeding? Is there broken skin? Does the site need to be cleaned with water and soap to remove debris? If it was a bee sting, can you see and remove the stinger? Do a thorough assessment before moving on.

 For simple cuts and scrapes, the most you need to do is clean the site with water and cover with a bandage. You can apply ointment to further protect the wound from infection. Sometimes you can get away with covering the site with ointment or petroleum jelly and letting it heal without putting any type of bandage on.

Burn and Sunburns: Burns can be caused by contact with fire, chemicals or electricity, smoke inhalation, hot water, or overexposing someone to the sun or other radiation. You must assess whether the burn is a first-degree, second-degree, or third-degree burn. First aid taken will depend on cause and severity of the burn.

First-degree burns can be treated by cooling them under cool, running water and applying cool, wet compresses until the pain stops. They can also be treated with skin care products like antibiotic ointment or aloe vera cream or gel, and pain medication. As they are mild and affect only the outer layer of skin (reddening and pain at most), there's no need for emergency medical attention. They're easy enough to deal with.

Second-degree burns affect the layers below the outer layer of skin (epidermis and dermis). Pain, redness, blistering and swelling are common. Remove tight items from the burned area, gently yet quickly, before swelling starts. Resist the urge to pop any blisters and loosely wrap the burn in a sterile gauze bandage. These burns may require an antibiotic cream or some other prescription ointment or cream. They are more painful than first-degree so the victim may wish to take some kind of medicine to ease the pain.

Third-degree burns are some of the most injuries you can get. These go through the dermis down to deeper tissues in the body. The site can have white or blackened, charred skin and flesh, and it may be numb due to nerve damage. This type of burn needs serious medical attention. The most you can do for first aid is to cover the burn with a sterile bandage or clean cloth to protect it. Don't try to remove any clothing that is stuck to the burn, and don't apply ointment or soak it in water.

First aid for burns will also vary depending on the location of the burns and whether a person has more than one. You may need to do first aid for second- and first-degree burns, one on the arm and one near the face, for example. Because the skin on the face is thinner in some spots than on the arm, and sometimes more sensitive, you need to adjust treatment to account for these differences.

Sprains and Broken Bones: A sprain is when a ligament (one of those tough, elastic-like bands of fiber connecting your bones and joints) is torn. This can be a partial tear or the ligament can be completely torn apart. These injuries are often painful and swell rapidly; the greater the pain and swelling, the worse the injury, as a general rule.

You'll want to avoid putting stress on the injury for a while. If it's a sprain in your knee or ankle, you'll probably need crutches to get around. Don't avoid all activity, though. You can still find ways to exercise or do work that don't put a lot of stress on the injury. After a day or two you can test to see if you can move the injured area without much pain. If not, the damage is probably worse than you first thought.

You can try icing the sprain to control swelling and pain, but more recent research has shown that after 48 to 72 hours, it is better to switch to heat treatment. The logic is that while ice eases pain and may stop swelling from getting worse, heat opens up blood vessels and relaxes muscles. This lets blood and fluid pass through more easily, which can help speed healing and reduce swelling.

You should still follow the advice of "20 minutes on, 20 minutes off." This means that you leave the hot or cold compress on for 20 minutes, and take it off for another 20 minutes. NOTE: Never put ice or a heat-pack directly on the skin, as this can cause damage. Use a thin towel or washcloth for protection.

Broken bones can result from a fall, an accident with tools, an attack from an animal, and so on. Sometimes it's hard to tell if a bone is broken, as the pain level may not be consistent with the severity of the fracture. So, look for these signs:

-Swelling or bruising over the site

-Deformity in a limb

-As mentioned, there may not be a lot of, but if it gets worse when pressure is applied or the area is moved, there may be a bone fracture

-Inability or bear weight on the affected leg, ankle, or foot

-Loss of function in the injured area

-If it is an open fracture (the bone shifts and starts poking through muscle and skin), the bone may pierce through the skin.

Wherever the broken bone is located, it is important to immobilize the area. If it's a broken leg, tie a splint on it and keep the leg still. A broken ankle should be comfortably secured and immobilized. A good option is to wrap the affected ankle in layers of clothing secured with bandages. If it's a broken arm, put a splint on it and then put it in a sling of some type. Make sure the arm is securely immobilized.

A broken hand should be wrapped in gauze to protect it from any more damage. A sling will elevate the injury and reduce swelling. Any broken fingers can be put in splints fashioned from tree bark or whatever you have available.

Broken ribs can be harder to treat, but again, the general idea is to secure the affected area so that the bone doesn't shift out of place. Same for a broken jaw. You may need to get creative with what materials you use and how you use them to keep the injury from getting worse.

You will have noticed that you are not supposed to move the broken bone, and may think this means the person should not move either.

You'd be right. However, if there is danger or if help has come but cannot easily reach the person, you will need to move them. Take care not to aggravate the injured area as you do so, though sometimes it can't be helped and the person will have to put up with some pain until they are in a safe location.

If you suspect a bone is broken in the head, back, or back, DO NOT move the person. The most you can do is immobilize the person and treat for shock if needed. This can mean you'll be stuck in one place until help arrives, but it's better than trying to move the person and risking paralysis or death.

WORST CASE SCENARIO: If the bone is broken such that it has come through muscle and skin, this is a very serious injury that calls for extra care. You must stop any bleeding by applying pressure with a sterile bandage, a clean piece of clothing or a clean cloth. Once you've done that, immobilize the injured area, but DO NOT try to realign the bone or push it back in. If you're trained in how to splint and professional help isn't immediately available, you can apply a splint above and below the site of the fracture. Put padding in the splints to help reduce discomfort. Apply ice packs to limit swelling and relieve pain. If the person shows signs of shock, begin treatment for that right away.

Shock: Shock is a serious condition that results from a sudden drop in blow flow through the body. It can be due to trauma, severe infection, blood loss, heatstroke, an allergic reaction, severe burns, poisoning, or something else. Shock prevents blood from flowing to organs, meaning those organs aren't getting enough oxygen. This can lead to permanent organ damage or worse, death.

Symptoms of shock will vary depending on the cause, but include:
-Nausea or vomiting
-Cool, clammy skin (due to excessive sweating)
-Rapid pulse

-Rapid breathing

-Weakness or fatigue

-Enlarged pupils

-Dizziness or fainting

-Pale or ashen skin

-Bluish tinge to lips or fingernails (in the case of dark complexions, look for a grayish tinge)

-Changes in behavior or mental status, such as agitation or anxiety.

Shock can be a sign of something else wrong, but even on its own, it is a serious condition requiring swift action. Lay the person down and raise the legs and feet slightly. This will encourage blood flow to the major organs, especially the heart. Don't do this if it will cause pain or further injury; another exception is if the person has a head injury, in which case you must raise the head and shoulders instead. This will help a lot if the person has difficulty breathing.

DO NOT let the person move, and do not try to move them unless absolutely necessary. Loosen tight clothes, and if needed, cover the person with a blanket to kepe them warm. Don't let them drink or eat anything.

If a person begins bleeding from the mouth or vomits, and you don't think there is a spinal injury, turn them onto their side to prevent choking. The worst-case scenario is if the person shows no signs of life, like coughing, breathing or moving. You must be CPR in that case.

If you can, get first-aid training. Even if you never have to use what you learn out in the wild, those skills can help you around the house, at school or work, or even when you're out with family or friends. Remember that you will have to judge for yourself what actions are best to take in an emergency, but never forget that the whole point of first aid is to ease pain and provide comfort, even when the situation is dire.

CHAPTER 11: How to Pack a Survival Kit

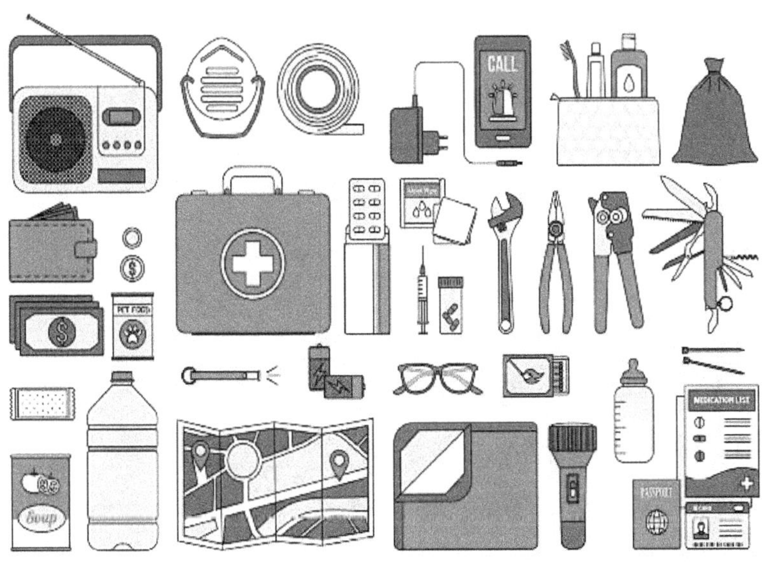

A survival kit is a great thing to have even if you don't make trips into the wilderness often. In the event of an emergency evacuation, that kit can mean the difference between misery and relative comfort. In the wilderness, a properly-stocked survival kit can mean the difference between life and death.

 should contain the following items:

- Fishing line
- Reflector
-Candle (not tallow, it can rot in hot weather)
-Matches
-Safety pins
-Thin wire
-Salt
-Fishing hooks and sinkers
-Adhesive bandages
-Magnifying glass
-Water purification tablets
-Antibiotics
-Needles, thread, and buttons
-Wire saw
-Plastic bag (or a biodegradable variety to be more eco-friendly)
-Pencil
-Scalpel
-Potassium Permanganate (useful for purifying water and fungal infections)

You can supplement these items with whatever is appropriate for where you live or plan to travel. Don't make the kit too heavy. Really think about what you need to include. Check the contents regularly to see if anything has expired and needs to be replaced.

Basic First Aid Kit

This kit should contain items which enable you to deal with most medical emergencies, helping you to stabilize a 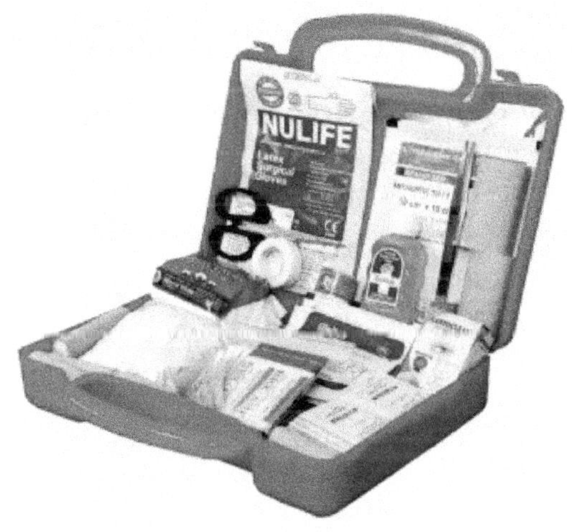 person until you can get them to a doctor. There are ready-made kits available, and indeed these often contain items which are very useful.

Assembling your own kit, though, lets you customize the contents depending your needs.

Whether you buy or make your own, a first-aid kit should have the following:

-Adhesive bandages (have a variety of sizes available if you like)
-Gauze padding
-Safety pins
-Gauze dressing and bandages
-Crepe and elastic bandages
-Painkillers
-Scissors
-Antiseptic
-Foot felt and corn pads
-Triangular bandage
-EpiPen or generic equivalent

Prescription medications, creams, and other medical supplies can be added as needed. It's a good idea to check the expiration dates on the items in your first-aid kit from time to time and replace ones which are past their expiration dates.

CHAPTER 12: 30 Amazing Outdoor Projects and Activities for Everyone, Everywhere

Looking for something fun to do outside during a hike or a walk in the park? We've compiled a list of fun activities and projects that you can do on your own or with a friend or family member.

1. Scavenger Hunt

Make a list of plants and animals to look for while you're outside, preferably with pictures so that everyone has a good idea of what to look for. If there are a lot of people playing, divide into teams. Let the goal of this activity be to simply enjoy and explore the great outdoors in the company of others – not every game has to have a prize to be fun! You can even take pictures of what you find and share them with everyone when the game is over.

2. How Many Do You See?

This is a simple counting activity that can be used ot help teach younger children to count, to name colors, and even teach children basic plant or animal identification. You can point to a flower and ask, "How many petals do you see?" If you find a small group of insects or fish, you can take turns guessing what type of fish or insect; once someone gets the right answer, say, "Great! How many do you see?"

3. Picnic and Photos

It's exactly what it sounds like: Pack up your favorite nibbles and drinks, packs your cameras (just use your phones) and have an outdoors photography session. Pick a location that is very accessible and has plenty of room for everyone in the group. Remember to bring sunscreen, umbrellas/parasols for those with extremely sensitive skin, and anything else that will make the outing fun for everyone. Photograph whatever you want, within reason (respect other people's privacy, please). You don't have to hold onto all the photos, or any at all. Those are mainly to teach children the importance of the "leave no trace" philosophy: Whatever you see out in nature, you don't touch it or try to take it home with you. Take a picture instead. Also, make sure that everyone pitches in to clean up after the picnic and photo shoot. This is another part of "leave no trace: philosophy: No one wants to see your leftovers or trash lying around. Pack it up and dispose of it properly.

4. Caterpillar Hunt

This is exactly what it sounds like. It works best if it's the right time of year and caterpillars are out and about. Use your phone or bring a nature book with you as you look for caterpillars. See how many you can identify.

5. HOMEMADE SUET BIRD FEEDER

This is a classic and fairly easy project that can be put together outdoors while you enjoy some nice weather! Suet is a type of fat that is used in cooking, but is also a real treat for birds. You can mix whatever birdseed, fruits, or insect bits into it you want. This will make it attractive to a wider range of birds.

If you're going to do this project during warm weather, try to find suet that's labeled as "no-drip," "no-melt," or "summer." These are rendered repeatedly to raise the melting point and make them more durable. Another tip is to place the suet in a shady area, away from direct sun – the birds will appreciate that you took the care to put their treat in such a nice spot!

To make the suet mixture, take your suet add-ins and mix them before pouring into molds (square cakes or logs are common shapes). Melt the suet down and pour over the mixture. Leave to harden at room temperature, or pop in the freezer for an hour or so.

Once the fat has hardened, remove from the molds. You may need to run the molds under warm water to loosen the suet mixture. You can make a hole to loop some twine through, or you may have picked up a wire cage to hold your suet mix. Either way, get your suet ready to go outside. Pick a good spot, place your suet, and soon enough you'll see the local birds coming to feast! See how many you can identify, and enjoy learning about any new birds.

6. BACKYARD CAMP OUT

As long as you've got a backyard, or a friend or relative will let you use theirs, you can still have fun with a backyard "camp out." No tent? That's fine – you can practice building a shelter from tarps, branches, or whatever other materials are available. Build a fire ring (but you don't need to start a real fire it if you don't want to/can't), set up the campsite like you would if you were really going camping. If there's snow, you can build trench shelters, or snow caves, etc. This "camp out" activity is meant to encourage you to practice important outdoor skills and have fun.

7. HIKING

A classic! You
don't need to
do some long,
daring trail at
the wildlife
preserve. Find
a place with

some nice easy trails, including wheelchair
accessible ones, and have fun exploring! Don't
forget to take pictures!

8. PADDLING

Paddle sports are a great option for people of all
ages and abilities (as long as they like the water).
Pick a place with calm waters if this will be your
first time. If there are experienced paddle sport
enthusiasts in your group, they can help people
who are just learning or those with disabilities if
they need it, paddle through somewhat more
exciting waters. Once you're all pretty
comfortable, you can try splitting up into pairs or
groups of three and going off on your own.

Make sure you pick watercraft that are in good shape, or bring your own if you have the room to store it and a vehicle to transport it. You may find some that are outfitted with outriggers to gives them more stability. These are great for people with disabilities or even if someone is a little too anxious about capsizing. You can even look for paddles made for people with reduced hand and wrist function if that's a concern.

9. COOKOUT/BBQ

Whether at your house, your grandparents' house, or a friend's house, a cookout can be loads of fun. Check to see if any local parks have spots specially-designated spots with BBQ pits. There may even be a local beach where they let you have cookouts!

Come to think of it, perhaps a way to expand on this is to get together with friends and family, pick some dates when you'd like to have a cookout or BBQ, and list some possible locations. People can pick the date and location they like, and everyone can take turns. Maybe by the end you'll have seen places you'd never have visited otherwise and made new friends.

10. PAINTING OUTDOORS

When it's a nice sunny day, or a cloudy day that's neither too cold nor too hot, why not having a painting session outdoors? A few tips:

-Use nontoxic paints, as much for the safety of any children involved as for the safety of any animals who may wander by. If you have pets and already have paints which are rated as safe to use around animals, you're set.

-Make sure you have plenty of supplies: brushes, paper towels or rags for cleanup, cups for water, etc.

-Smocks or old t-shirts for wearing over your clothes. You don't have to get dressed up for this activity, but it makes cleanup (and laundry day) easier if you can avoid getting paint on your clothes.

-Pick a good spot, preferably one that's near shade or in the shade, and set up your painting supplies. If you have an easel that can be set on a table, now's the time to get that out. Otherwise you can place your painting surface flat on a table.

-Paint whatever you like. If you want to try painting a picture of those lovely flowers near the back door, go ahead. Feel like painting that weird animal you saw in a dream the other night? Sure! Just feel like putting dabs and streaks of color on paper with no real plan? Wonderful, go ahead!

-Don't worry about painting a perfect picture. The point of this is to have fun!

-If you want, you can make this a party! Invite friends, have some snacks and drinks, and paint to your hearts' content.

11. SNOW CASTLE

This is a group activity, so get some friends or family members together. You can either sketch out what you want the castle to look like beforehand, or you can just start building and see what happens. Take plenty of pictures to share and celebrate your new castle, no matter how silly! More fun: when you want to building something else or just are bored with the castle, grab your gloves and boots, and a snow shovel or two, and demolish it! Then go inside and have something hot to drink.

12. WALKING TOUR

Lots of cities and towns offer walking tours.
Some visit haunted places, some just visit
important buildings and other landmarks, and
some will even take you out into the woods. See
what your hometown has to offer, or if there's a
tour at a nearby location that sounds interesting.
Check to see how long the tour is supposed
to last. If there's time left in the day, consider
getting a bite to eat on the way home. If your
tour is at night, make sure to eat before you
meet the tour guide. Also take into account if
you or someone in your group needs to take
medication at a certain time, or needs other
accommodations in order to make the tour
enjoyable. Come prepared in case the weather
turns foul.

13. MAKE YOUR OWN WALKING TOUR

Let's face it: Tours can be fun, but sometimes
they only go to the well-known places that
everyone already knows. If you want to step
outside those established routes, why not plan
your own walking tour? Think of any places you
may have been curious about, or that are

supposed to have interesting stories attached to them. If there are none where you live, why not check out what's in the next city or town?

This requires research and lots of planning (will you walk there or take the bus? Drive and then walk? Will you need to take breaks so someone with problems walking or breathing can have some relief? What about snacks?), so asking an adult to help would be a good idea. If you can come up with a very workable, and walker-friendly, plan that everyone likes, well done! Pick a date and time, and another date and time in case of bad weather on the first try. Make sure everyone who wants to go has those dates blocked off so that no other plans interfere.

When you go on your tour, don't be afraid to use a smartphone to look up interesting facts about the landmarks and other locations you visit. Maybe the locals have stories to share, too. While you're walking around, enjoy the scenery in between locations. Smell the flowers. Marvel at how pretty the sunset is. Admire the trees changing color or putting out their spring buds and blossoms. Take time to play, too!

14. KITES, KITES, AND MORE KITES

Kites come in a variety of shapes, sizes, and colors. You can buy one, or find instructions online or in a book (check the library to see if they have any) for how to make your own. Making your own kite could be turned into a fun outdoor project itself, especially if your friends or family join in and in the process make their kites, too.

Once you have your kite, check the weather and pick a day to go fly it. You want a day with some wind, but not too much, so the kite doesn't get damaged and the string doesn't get ripped out of your hands. Kites can be flown on a cloudy day or a clear day. This activity is probably best saved for when there's no snow on the ground (although if you want to see if it's doable in the winter, be my guest.)

Pick a location where there is lots of room and there aren't a lot of trees. If you want to make a day of it, bring some snacks or a proper picnic, set up a spot at a table, on a blanket, or under some trees. When the wind is just right, time to fly that kite!

15. DAY AT THE BEACH

This doesn't need a lot of explanation. As long as
you or someone else isn't allergic to fish (some
people's allergies are so bad they can't even walk
on the sand at a beach), this is a good way to
spend a late spring or summer day. Whether you
bring something to eat or not depends on how
long you're going to be there. That being said,
some beaches have grills or other such equipment
that you can use to cook burgers, chicken,
vegetables, etc. Build a sand castle (see how big
you can make it), see how many different types
of shells you can find, look for fish and other sea
life in tide pools. Explore and enjoy!

16. BICYCLE TOUR

Find out if
there's a trail
that's bicycle
friendly.
Decide if you
want to make
this a short
trip, or if

you'd like to make it a longer one and take a bag lunch or some snacks. On a day that's just right (preferably without rain or other weather that would make the trip very uncomfortable – extreme heat also falls into this category), grab your bike, maybe meet some friends at the trail, and spend your time checking out the scenery, people watching, even explore a town that you haven't been to before. Just remember to stay on or close to the trail because that's how you're going to get home. If you brought snacks or a proper lunch, remember to take a break to eat and rest. It's fun to ride your bike around, but you've got to hold onto some energy for the trip home!

17. OUTDOORS – FOR SCIENCE!

While some science experiment are fine for indoors, there are plenty which are better suited for outdoors. This can be because they are very messy, or use chemicals and other materials that are not safe to use indoors. The problem is that these experiments can be the most fun ones to perform!

Pick a day when the weather Is nice and go through some science experiments online or in a book. Choose one or two that seem like fun, and make sure there's an adult or two to help you. Get the equipment you need.

Let's stop here and go over proper safety gear. You may be going outdoors, but that's no excuse for not protecting yourself.

-Safety goggles
-Gloves
-Face masks. You might want to consider buying something that's a bit more heavy-duty than the soft face masks that only keep out dust, pollen, smoke and bacteria. Otherwise you make do with what you have and use extra caution around anything that the masks aren't rated for.
-Something to wear over your clothes to protect them. Make sure it's something you can bear to see get turned into a ragged, stained mess.
-Footwear. Depending on what's involved you may want to swap your sneakers for something heavier so that your feet are better protected. It hurts to drop something heavy right on your toes!
-Spares of all your safety gear.

Once you've got your safety gear on, it's time to experiment! Reassure your neighbors if there happens to a be long bang or two and they get concerned that something is wrong. Tell them you have an adult supervising and thank them for their concern.

Also, have an emergency contact who you can call in the event that you need assistance or need a ride to get medical treatment. Science can be fun, but sometimes even with the right safety and precautions, you can still get hurt.

Don't forget to clean up when you're done. As with camping, leave no trace!

18. RAIN CATCHER

Rain is water and life on Earth is very much dependent on water. It's so important that we will go so far as to measure how much rainfall we get. This would make a fun little project to do on a rainy day, as it doesn't require anyone to be outside for long.

Take a glass jar or a clean, empty can (save one from when your family makes dinner) and measure 1-inch increments with a ruler. Mark these increments with a permanent marker and set the can or jar outside. Note the time that you left the jar outside. Leave it alone for a few minutes and then check to see how much water is in it. Repeat this every once in a while, until the rain stops. You may want to mark up a couple of extra jars or cans in case it looks like the rain will be falling for a long time. Once the rain stops, or just before you go to bed, see how much is in the jar(s.). Note the time you stopped the experiment and how much rain fell.

If you had to use extra jars, make sure you note the total from each jar.

19. PUDDLE EXPLORATION

After a good rainfall, it can be fun to pull on your boots and raincoat and go outside to splash in puddles and see if any interesting animals have come out. If you live in an area where frogs are common, you might find a few enjoying themselves in the puddles left behind from the rain. Using a cup, you can scoop water from puddles to see what's in it (pour the water back in after you're done). If you have a microscope at home, you might want to take a few samples of water and look at a drop or two under your microscope. Believe it or not, puddles can be treasure troves of life! Have a book or a smartphone next to you so you can check which lifeforms you're seeing.

You may even, when taking your water samples, find a tadpole or two in your cup! These wriggly little cuties are the baby stage of a frog's life. It's not advisable to take them home as pets, so after you're done marveling over the tadpoles, please put them back in the water.

20. SIDEWALK CHALK "PAINTINGS"

Drawing on the sidewalk with chalk is an activity thank many kids enjoy, and some adults too. Did you know that you can "paint" with sidewalk chalk and a bit of water? You can do these one of two ways.

You can make your pictures, words, etc. on the sidewalk with chalk. Then take a small container of water, and using your hands or a brush, wipe the water over the chalk. Play around and see how different colors look when mixed with water, or see if you can create a new picture with the "paint" you've made.

The second way is to wait until after it stops raining, then grab your sidewalk chalk and go outside to draw. If it rains again, don't worry.

You can go back outside and redo your art, or make something new.

21. LAZY RIVER TUBING

River tubing is a low-impact activity that requires very little equipment. You may have heard stories about people grabbing a bunch of old car or truck inner tubes and heading to the nearest river. Nowadays you can find floating tubes (also known as "donuts") in a variety of colors and patterns for sale. Some are true donuts, with a hole in the center where your butt will make contact with the water. Some have a panel inserted across the hole to keep rocks on the river bottom from popping up and injuring the rider when they venture into shallow water areas. These don't usually have handles, but look around for one if you would prefer something of that design.

Find out about nearby rivers which are used for tubing and other water activities. Learn if they have any shallow spots, or dangerous parts that you should avoid. If you or someone else needs floaties in case of tipping over, make sure to bring those when you make that trip to the river for a relaxing few hours, or a day, on the water.

22. HOBBY ROCKETS

Hobby rockets are fun to build and fun to set off so they fly high in the air. It's an activity that doesn't require a lot of moving around, but it does call for patience, as model rockets can have parts that are small and tough to position just so. You also need plenty of space to work, especially if you want to build more than one. There are a range of model kits you can buy. They're a fun little project for people who love building things and for physics enthusiasts.

23. BIRDING

Remember the suet feeder? Besides being a food source for birds during the winter, it can also attract species that you may not see often – which makes your backyard a great place to go birding! Grab a pair of binoculars, or just set yourself with a chair, some refreshments, and maybe an umbrella to protect yourself from the sun. Enjoy watching all the birds as they come to feast. Have a bird guidebook or a website open on your smartphone to help you identify the ones you see. You can even go birding at the park.

24. GEOCACHING

This is a relative newcomer to the world of outdoor activities. It's not unlike a treasure hunt, in that you have to find something while moving around outside, sometimes going into unfamiliar areas. That's where handheld GPS devices come in: Geocachers visit one of many geocaching sites to find the coordinates for a cache. Plug these coordinates into your device, grab a backpack of supplies, and away you go! When you find the cache (called "swag"), you take the logbook that's left with it to record your name and details of your trip. You can even do this part online. You return the logbook and cache to the spot where you found it, so that other geocachers can try their luck. While the cache may not hold anything of high value, you may find one that has some unusual items in it. If you find something you'd like to take, you must leave something of similar or higher value in its place.

25. SNOWSHOEING

This is a form of hiking that started out as a mode of transportation and has become something of a hobby. The most expensive equipment you'll need is a good pair of snowshoes (best bet is to try them before you buy, to make sure they fit your feet properly). Poles for helping you move and keep your balance are optional. It's a low-impact form of exercise that people of all ages can enjoy.

26. FORAGING/BERRY PICKING

Berry picking can be done on a farm, where you pay a fee to fill up as many containers as you can (or are allowed to – some places may have a limit) with berries. If done in the wild, it falls under the category of "foraging." This requires some knowledge of what safe, edible plants are in your area. Of course, if you're lucky enough to have berries growing in your backyard, or on the property of someone you have a good relationship with, then you can enjoy this outdoor activity without having to wander very far at all. You can forage for mushrooms, but as mentioned elsewhere in this book, it can be hard to tell if a species is safe to eat or not. If you are determined to try, find someone who knows a lot about mushrooms (you can look for forgaging group to join online – these are made up of people who have been doing this for a while and can be super helpful) and make the trip with them. When you forage in the wild, it's best to go with a group and bring a map or some kind of navigation device so you can reduce your chances of getting lost on the way back to your car.

27. SNOW TUBING

If you haven't got a sled and there's plenty of snow on the ground, snow tubing might be an option. Some ski resorts are open to tubing, but it can be just as fun to slide down a hill near your house or at the park. Make sure you wear the right clothes (snow pants and a proper winter jacket or coat are recommended), and if you go with family and friends, consider having a little get-together afterwards with lots of warm drinks and good things to eat.

28. SQUIRREL WATCHING

It's like bird watching, but with squirrels. HINT: If you have a bird feeder or a suet feeder set up, chances are you'll see squirrels visiting to grab some food, too. They can be fun to watch, even if they do make a mess of the yard by tipping over feeder by accident or on purpose.

29. ROCK HUNTING

Sometimes you pick up a rock and take it home just because it looks pretty. However, some people will focus on collecting only certain types of rocks, or gemstones, even fossils. You don't need to even know much about rocks to start – you'll learn a lot as you start searching for and collecting for whatever specimens you find most interesting. For equipment, you'll need a backpack, a rock, a shovel, gloves, a chisel, a hammer, and containers or wrapper to put your rocks in. Maps and a guidebooks about rocks and minerals would be helpful too.

30. TAI CHI

All right, so this isn't strictly an outdoors activity. There's something to be said, however, for practicing this gentle martial art outside where you can enjoy the sun and a cool breeze. If you practice in a group, you might find the class heading to a park or nature reserve on a clear, sunny day (hopefully it's not too hot or too cold out). With the chirping of birds, perhaps the quiet burbling of a river or stream, as background music, you may find yourself wishing you could practice tai chi outdoors more often.

THANK YOU

who have been doing this for a while and can be super helpful) and make the trip with them. When you forage in the wild, it's best to go with a group and bring a map or some kind of navigation device so you can reduce your chances of getting lost on the way back to your car.

27. SNOW TUBING

If you haven't got a sled and there's plenty of snow on the ground, snow tubing might be an option. Some ski resorts are open to tubing,but it can be just as fun to slide down a hill near your house or at the park. Make sure you wear the right clothes (snow pants and a proper winter jacket or coat are recommended), and if you go with family and friends, consider having a little get-together afterwards with lots of warm drinks and good things to eat.

28. SQUIRREL WATCHING

It's like bird watching, but with squirrels. HINT: If you have a bird feeder or a suet feeder set up, chances are you'll see squirrels visiting to grab some food, too. They can be fun to watch,